THE
GREAT WALL
OF CHINA

Photography ROLAND and SABRINA MICHAUD

Text MICHEL JAN

Translated from the French by JOSEPHINE BACON

| ABBEVILLE PRESS PUBLISHERS | New York | London |

FOR THE ENGLISH EDITION

Editor: Susan Costello

Cover designer: Julietta Cheung

Interior typographic designer:
   Barbara Sturman

Production editor: Ashley Benning

Production manager: Louise Kurtz

English translator: Josephine Bacon

Book designer: François Chevret

First edition
10 9 8 7 6 5 4 3 2 1

LIBRARY OF CONGRESS CATALOGING-IN-PUBLICATION DATA

Michaud, Roland.
   [Grande muraille de Chine. English]
   The great wall of China / Photography: Roland & Sabrina Michaud; text: Michel Jan.
      p. cm.
   Includes bibliographical references and index.
   ISBN 0-7892-0736-2 (alk. paper)
   1. Great Wall of China (China) I. Michaud, Sabrina.
   II. Jan, Michel. III. Title.

DS793.G67 M5313 2001
951—dc21   2001022732

CONTENTS

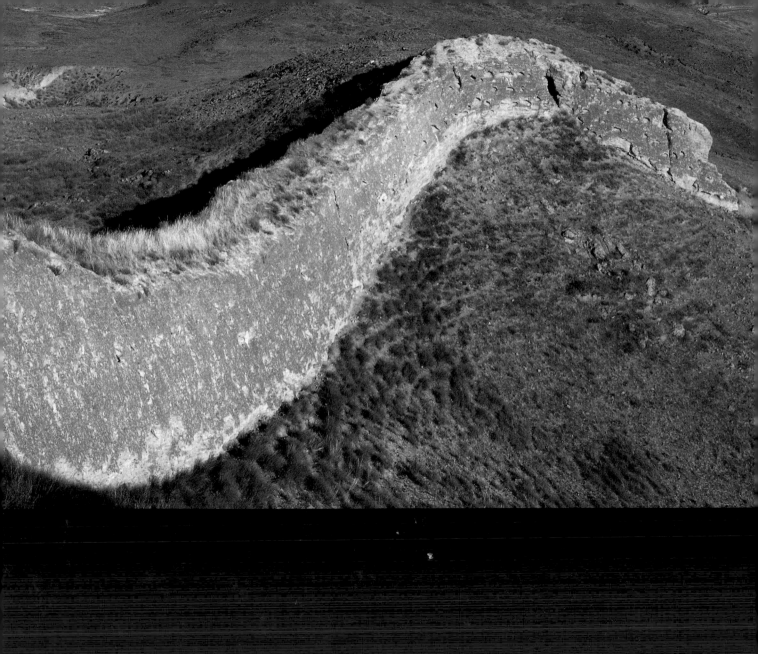

Compacted earth section of the Great Wall at Bataicun, north of Datong, Shanxi Province.

"I had no reason to transpose the image I had of it," wrote Auguste Gilbert de Voisins, a member of Victor Segalen's party, when, in July 1909, he first came upon the section of the Great Wall at the Juyong-guan (Juyong Pass),[1] which had been built during the Ming dynasty. "I saw it the way I wanted to see it. Farther on (but what did I care!), it diminished, being reduced to a mere mud wall; even farther away, it had disappeared in places, obliterated by the desert winds; a few isolated towers in the vast plain, a few gates, were the only reminders of where it had once stood. Despite all this, I can still admire it in all its monstrous splendor. It imposes, it astonishes, it fires the imagination. It is a long poem in brick and stone, composed by human hands, its meanderings following the contours of the living landscape in its abrupt twists and turns, as if it were part of Nature. This gigantic serpent emerges from the ocean beside a bare beach, forges its way across the plain, crawls up mountainsides, scales peaks, and plunges into ravines, only to reemerge on the other side. Nothing stops it, nothing gets in its way; seeing it at this point, one might believe it to be eternal. All the caravans that pass slowly through its gates and even the wildflowers, ephemeral and naive decoration beside the road

THE ORIGIN AND SYMBOLISM OF THE WALL

Dragon, multicolored wood   13

that snakes over the crest, merely add to the impression of eternity that it conveys.

"From the time when Huangdi linked those fragments that had already been built, from the days when he would condemn to death a careless workman who left the tiniest breach in his work, one barely large enough to hold a nail, from the day when this massive thing was complete, it took twenty-one centuries to destroy just a few sections of it.

"I see its mighty structure and sinuous line stretching before me across the land; the towers that loom up to confront me, though they dwindle into tiny dots on distant peaks, never cease their vigilance, and they remain forbidding. For a moment, I try to imagine the wall as being whole once more, crossing space and time, from Shanhai-kuan [Shanhaiguan] to the Gobi Desert, from the day on which Genghis Khan first broke through it, right up to the present day.

"A magnificent monument that defies attempts to understand it, a belt wrapped around a continent, a grand design, a plan fulfilled, one of the major defense lines of the world, the incredible dream of an emperor, the chimera of a moment turned into an immutable stone dragon—that is the ten-thousand-*li* Wall, the Great Wall of China!"[2]

FROM A FRAGMENTARY VISION and a shared dream, a mythical wall was born that transcends reality. In this respect, the Great Wall is the perfect representation, the multifaceted image of constructions created in the mind, the stuff that dreams are made of. Approaching this rampart for the first time, at the point where it is built of stone, the visitor feels certain of having seen it before. With a lazy complicity, he enthuses about its size, delights in its existence. The visitor climbs the steps of a tower, from which to contemplate the distant hills. He is immediately confronted with another world, another era. In a single glance, the eye can sweep across the marvel—or monstrosity—that runs from the shores of the Pacific to the deserts of central Asia. Certainty and complicity combine when feelings run wild before this overwhelming apparition. It is the culmination and combination of a long succession of dynasties, chronicles and legends, fabulous beasts and the race for conquest. The wall is firstly that which we imagine—its reality and the void that it conceals, the past that has been created for it and the future that awaits it. It is a terrifying sight that embraces every corner of Chinese history, the cold, implacable authority of the empire, the legions of those banished beyond its frontiers, exile to the gateway to the desert, the clash of arms on the field of battle—this series of vivid living tableaux is played out against the background of the Great Wall.

After the Qin dynasty, almost every succeeding dynasty built walls along the northern frontier. The most spectacular of these fortifications, however, the symbols of the huge scale of the defensive action against the turbulent barbarians of the north—Xiongnu, Xianbei, Turks, Nuzhen (Djurchet), Mongols, and Manchus—were built under the Han dynasty, between the second century B.C.E. and the second century C.E., and under the Ming dynasty, between the fifteenth and sixteenth centuries. A section of the wall may have been remodeled or reinforced under a particular dynasty, but most of the lines of fortifications, especially those of the Han and Ming, are distinctive in style. Despite this fact, the image persists of a unified, continuous wall, linked to the origins of imperial China, authoritatively replacing the reality, a multitude of ramparts constructed over a period of two thousand years.

Here, on either side of the wall, without any apparent discontinuity, nations have confronted each other, enriched by their differences and their interaction, each full of hatred and pitiless ambition, leading to the ultimate frontiers of their lives. Separation, exile, and death, with all their sufferings and lamentations, have inspired historians and poets over the centuries. The ghosts of the Great Wall's victims still haunt it, whether in sections of a high wall, vague undulations in the midst of modern human habitation, or barely visible traces of an embankment or earthwork.

The Wall is being built, with raucous cries
*   and groans;*
The Moon and Milky Way seem low in
*   comparison.*
But if the white bones of the dead were not
*   removed,*
They would rise as high as the top of the
*   Great Wall.*

—Lu Yu, "Song of the Frontiers"[3]

It is time to perform one of those pirouettes and somersaults that make the Beijing Opera so enthralling. So long a wailing wall, the Great Wall has been turned into the very symbol of modern China, thanks to the efforts of the present rulers. "Love China. Help rebuild the Great Wall!" Fascination and phantoms have overturned history and the present in an eternal China, a boundless, lugubrious reality engorged with myths.

The Great Wall at Jinshanling
Camel drover, terra-cotta figurine of the Tang dynasty

A SACRED SQUARE WAS TRADI-
tionally used to represent the empire and, before it, the kingdom. It enclosed other walled
enclosures, those of the principalities. These
in turn contained walled cities, walled fields, and
closed encampments. These living areas were designed to mirror the principles that governed the
distribution of groups of humanity. The world is a
closed universe. The idea of an undefined expanse
is troubling and disquieting. A restricted space, enclosed by a wall, is reassuring. Unity is a prerequi-
site within such a boundary. When a wall is broken
down and rebuilt amid agitation, no compartment
or institution exists to oppose the propagation of
new forces within the vast enclosure.

The context in which life is lived demands
a cautious approach. The geomancers, masters of
feng shui, make choices about the environment in
its widest sense. Does it favor those benevolent
spirits that are capable of repelling evil genies?
Central to the art is the north-south axis, one that
is not merely symbolic since it combines a princi-
ple of order with a genuine, historical experience.
The northern Mongolian plateau is responsible
for the harsh winds of winter as well as the barbarian invasions. Human dwellings must there-
fore turn their back to the north, just as the Great
Wall blocks the route of the invaders.

Such bitter, austere landscapes have always
produced men and women who are able to accli-
matize to the rigors of nature. The northern Chinese have become accustomed to simple ideas
and a difficult existence. The northerner is tall,
strong, healthy, good-natured, and jovial; he likes
eating onions; he is kind and sincere, open and
straightforward. In other words, he is more Mongolian and more traditional than the inhabitants
of the vast population centers around Shanghai,
and the hills and deltas of southern China.

THE FARMLAND AND PASTURES
of the north eventually give way to grassy
plateaus, uplands, and steppes. The history
of northern China is a succession of pulsations, of conquests and withdrawals. A dynasty
is founded at the frontier or beyond it and takes
over the whole of China; or it is born in China
but, to dominate and control, it has to extend its
hegemony to the frontier or beyond.

The Yan Shan (Yan Mountains), the mountains of Shanxi, and the Hexi[4] steppe all present
stark contrasts to the gentle, undulating landscape of southern China. Almost all the founders
of the great dynasties emerged from these frontier lands beside the desert, or from the plains and
valleys north of the Yellow River basin. At first
they were vagabonds with a warlike spirit, sav-
ages who happened to possess the qualities of
leadership. Only once they had occupied the
throne of the empire did they begin to educate
themselves and take an interest in the teachings
of Confucius,which provided the justification for
an implacable order that favored their iron rule.

From the steppes of Manchuria to the gates
of Turkestan, the boundaries extend like a taut
bow stretched toward traditional China. Even
today, such spaces remain to be conquered, protected, and defended. This is the theater of rival-

Preceding pages: Encampment on the Mongolian steppe

ries and confrontations—but also of interaction. Other civilizations and cultures—Greek, Roman, Indian, Persian, Turkish, Mongolian, and Russian—have insidiously attempted to influence China and have tried to invade it. This hostile terrain has isolated China and protected it from such incursions. The soil here is poor and cannot support a large population. Where, exceptionally, a region does lend itself to heavier population density, such as the southern fringes of Mongolia or the plain of Manchuria, the Han[5] Chinese were brought in to overwhelm and outnumber the native Mongols or the more recently arrived inhabitants of Russian origin.[6]

The Great Wall is not a single entity but a multitude of stone ramparts and embankments that zigzag crazily, snaking beside a long ridge or a loess escarpment, hugging the tortuous topography of the north and the vast, empty expanses of the west. In their various forms as barriers, many of which have worn away with time, these walls are not merely a line running along the western end of the country in a long arc almost eighteen hundred miles (2,900 km) long from the western extremity of Gansu to the Korean frontier. More than three hundred miles (484 km) of it reflect the various attempts by successive dynasties to contain the barbarians, from north to south, from the Mongolian border (the wall built by the Jin dynasty) to the southern slopes of the Yan Shan range (the Ming walls). China was a civilization that vacillated for centuries, in a vain attempt to find where its true boundaries lay.

Such open spaces, on the fringes of two worlds, are an invitation to conquest by those on either side. The vast expanses and the wild and savage nature of the inhabitants, their racehorses, and the biting winds of the steppe inspire action or songs of freedom. Emperor Chenwu of the Northern Qi would shed tears when he heard the "Song of the Chele," written by Huliu Qin, a champion horseman:

Beside the Chele, at the foot of the Yin Mountains [7]
The sky, like a yurt, covers the four corners of
*   the plain,*
The sky is blue, blue,
The plain huge, huge.
When the wind blows and the grass bends,
One espies cattle and sheep.[8]

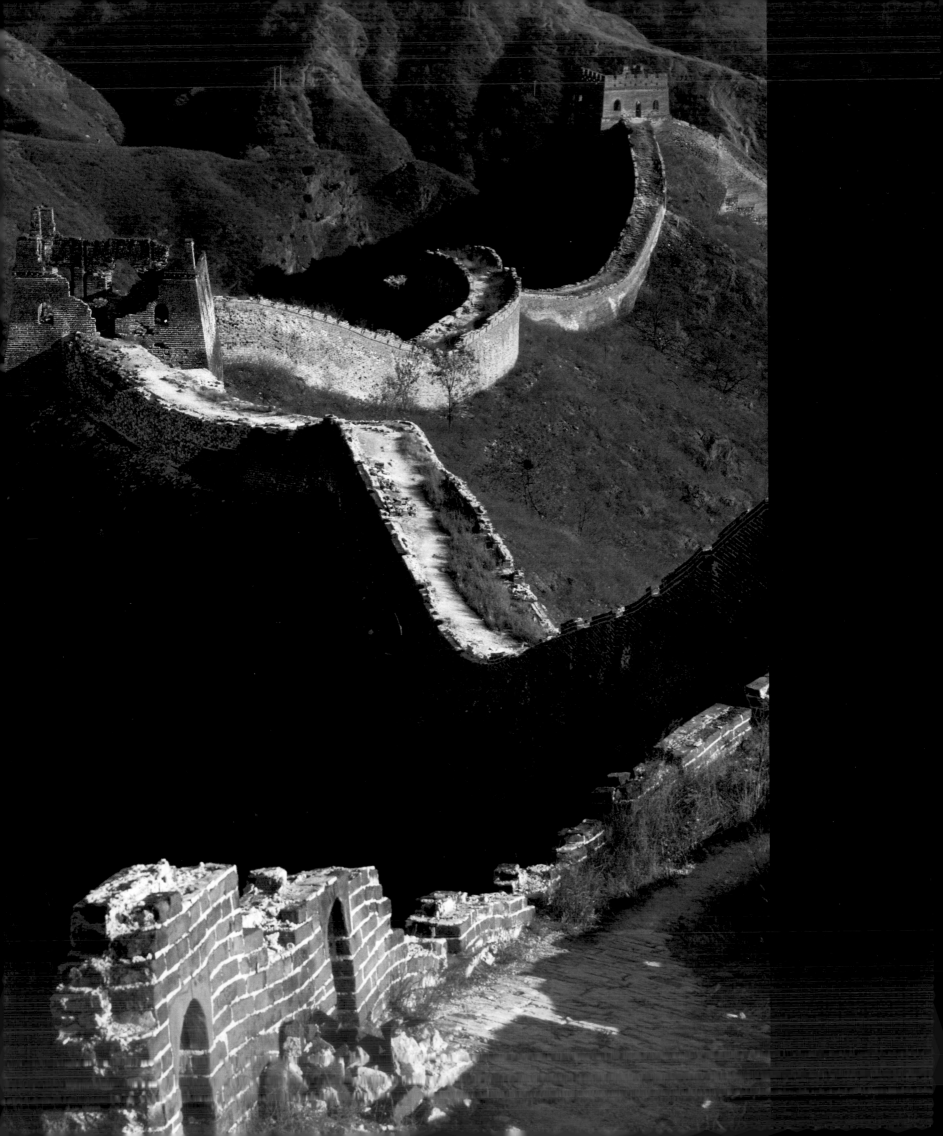

These short verses, so naive in content, are drawn directly from the dismal landscapes of the north, and contrast with the reveries produced in the south, whose supple, delicate contours have produced lyrics typical of the Song dynasty (1127–1279), in which wilting characters languish in melancholy and sadness:

The time of the perfumes has passed, but the Lake
*   of the West[9] retains all its beauty.*
Here and there a few tufts of pink linger on:
Fluffy catkins wave in the air.
The breeze stirs the long branches of the weeping
*   willows.*[10]

Such a people expected to be dominated by a population more inclined to action, such as this "prince of Langye," from the time of the Liang, another dynasty that originated in the north. These lines are dedicated unequivocally, to the accompaniment of traversing flutes and barbaric cornets, to a newly acquired sword:

The five-foot blade that I have just bought
Is hung on the pillar in the center.
Three times a day I caress it,
Much more than I would a fifteen-year-old girl.[11]

Here, at the very edge of the world that farmers from the Chinese interior considered to be the limits of farmland, the walls were erected. Those who dared venture beyond their confines had to disperse in order to survive. They lived in the turmoil of a "land beyond the pale" that disturbed their peace of mind. Anyone unlucky enough to die there could not rest in peace. Families stored coffins in the temples, in the hope that the wanderer would return and funds could be collected for the purpose of transporting the body back to the province of birth, in the interior. When the time came, hearse after hearse bore caskets toward the Great Wall. On each was a cage containing a rooster, preferably a white one. The crowing of the bird was supposed to keep the spirit of the dead person awake until the divide had been crossed. Otherwise, it was feared that the spirit would escape, wander, and forget its body, which would thus be abandoned beside the Great Wall.

IN THE SEVENTH CENTURY B.C.E., it appears that among the federations centering around a powerful chieftain fighting the surrounding barbarians, a sense of pride in being Chinese was born. This superiority implied a form of organization. This is when the walls were first constructed as a defense against the barbarians, those "wolves of insatiable avidity." The first time these structures are mentioned is in 658 or 656 B.C.E., in what are now the provinces of Henan and Hebei.[12]

A fiefdom originally consisted of a walled city. The city itself was surrounded by a ring of cultivated fields, protected by more walls. At the outskirts of the Chinese civilized world, the overlords extended the boundaries of their land and contained the unassimilated barbarians by constructing new walls. These fortifications multiplied around the first city-states, concentrated in the central and lower valley of the Yellow River.

The purpose of the walls was mainly to defend the overlords from barbarians who were encouraged to attack them by rival landowners. Seven sovereign states or kingdoms emerged from the battles that took place during the period of the so-called Fighting Kingdoms (475–221 B.C.E.). These were Qin, Qi, Chu, Han, Zhao, Wei, and Yan. Vestiges of the walls built in this period can still be seen in most of the provinces of northern China, including Hubei, Shanxi, Shaanxi, Shandong, Henan, Hebei, Liaoning, and Inner Mongolia.

Leaping horse, Tang dynasty terra-cotta
Lassoing a horse, Mongolia

THE FIRST
EMPIRE AND
THE FIRST
GREAT WALL

History and tradition, reinforced by legend, are full of irony. They grant the first emperor, Qin Shi Huangdi, a tyrant who reigned from 259 to 210 B.C.E. and who was held in contempt by the generations of cultured rulers who followed him, the accolade of having unified China (in 221). He is credited with fathering the Great Wall, and from his name comes the name by which his country is known outside its borders—China.[13] The construction of the Great Wall is mentioned gloomily by the great historian Sima Qian[14] in a chapter devoted to the biography of one of the generals of the first imperial dynasty. The biography states that when Qin had unified everything under the heavens, Meng Tian was given the command of an army of 300,000 men to go northward, repel the Rong and Di barbarians,[15] and seize the territories south of the Yellow River. He built the Great Wall, taking advantage of the topography of narrow gorges and mountain passes. It extended from Lintao[16] in the west to Liaodong[17] in the east, a distance of more than ten thousand *lis*. After crossing the Yellow River, it followed the line of the Yan Shan (the Yan Mountains) and then turned north. The army withstood the rigors of the terrain in Shang Province for ten years. Throughout this time, Meng Tian terrorized the Xiongnu.[18]

Turkish or Mongolian prisoner, fifteenth-century miniature

The Great Wall at Jinshanling

The state of China and the first Great Wall were founded simultaneously by the emperor. They thus remained inseparable from each other, ancient and patched, imposing and passive, but eternal and imperial.

Terrorization was converted into a system of government, and spread among all of Qin's subjects. He banished tens of thousands of exiles to the northern frontiers and employed hundreds of thousands of forced laborers to work on building the imperial tomb, "three superimposed hills" stamped on the valley like a wax seal, guarded by a countless underground army of terra-cotta soldiers, among the first of many notable discoveries.[19]

Measures taken to unify the empire were accompanied by excesses of tyrannical power. As owner of all the land known under heaven, the ferocious master of the living, the first emperor even tried to tame death and used his furnaces to cook the drug, edible gold, the wine of joy that creates immortals.[20] He favored the Taoists and the elixir of youth, burned ancient books, and exterminated Confucian scholars.

The Confucians drew satisfaction from learning of the end reserved for the builder of the wall of Qin. "There is a crime," admitted Meng Tian, builder of the wall, "for which I should certainly have been killed. I built a wall of more than ten thousand *lis* from Lintao to Liaodong, and over such an expanse I must inevitably have severed the arteries of the earth. That is my crime." He immediately took poison and died.[21] Sima Qian, the merciless judge, witnesses his own quest through the land in his memoirs: "I traveled from the northern frontier. . . . During the course of my journey I saw the ramparts of the Great Wall that Meng Tian had built for Qin. He had dug out mountains, spanned valleys, and opened a direct route. Assuredly, he had no concern for the exertions of his subjects. Qin had destroyed the feudal states, but the spirits of men under the heaven had not yet found tranquillity, the wounded were not healed. Yet even though he had become a famous general, [Meng Tian] never used his position to remonstrate with his overlord or help alleviate the distress of the people, see to the needs of the elderly, enable the orphans to survive, or do everything in his power to cultivate harmony among the masses. Instead, he complacently served imperial ambitions. Consequently, was it not fitting that he and his brother suffered the death penalty?"

NORTH OF THE WEI RIVER Valley,[22] from which Chinese civilization first emerged and where the first emperor established his capital, lies the Ordos, a region that has played an important role throughout Chinese history. The area is bounded on three sides by a huge meander of the Yellow River, and on the fourth, the south, by a wall erected by King Chaoxiang of Qin (third century B.C.E.), an ancestor of the first emperor, Qin Shi Huangdi. These are austere lands, traditionally populated by nomads, but they have a strange fascination. In the evening the deserted plateau of the Ordos, gray and red during the day, is shrouded in a violet mantle. Along with the scorched boulders of the desert and the sand of the dunes, the grass of the steppes, the *sighi*, undulates farther than the eye can see. The thick, tough stems of this grass sometimes grow as high as a man on horseback. Between these tufts of grass grow large clumps of a small, white-flowered shrub whose fruits resemble pomegranate seeds. Beside the river the ground is fertile and can be irrigated, making it suitable for crops. Nowhere else is there such a contrast of barren soil and rich earth. It seems as though since time immemorial, mud walls have been erected to keep the peoples of the steppe at bay. It is here that Prince Wuling of Zhao, a district of the Ordos, who lived in the fourth century B.C.E., borrowed from the barbarian horsemen the tactic of using light bowmen on horseback. The cultural exchanges went far beyond copying military strategies. To fight on equal terms, the Chinese not only adopted the cavalry but also the narrow breeches of the horsemen, as well as their harnesses, buckles, and other riding tackle.

The feudal period that lasted until the empire was united in 221 B.C.E. saw much cultural influence of the art of the steppes on Chinese art. The result was the production of the so-called Ordos bronzes.[23] Knives, daggers, battle-axes, hatchets, harnesses, belt buckles, spearheads, and decorative items are covered with representations of animals, their outlines spare or elaborate, distorted or expanded into a huge field of fantasy. There are bronzes in the shape of horses and deer, generally in pairs or clenched in the jaws or claws of tigers or bears, in a range of possibilities unequaled in animal art. Decorative patterns originating from central Asia and hitherto unknown to the Chinese or disliked by them—plants, droplets, circles, commas, triangles—entered Chinese art during the feudal period, introduced by their nomadic neighbors.

That these influences preceded countercurrents originating in China that returned in different forms merely emphasized the importance of this interaction between different nations.

More generally, this northern border, open to foreigners who were so very different, was constantly disrupting the plans and interfering with the interests of the centralized Chinese state, which strived to exclude anything that could not be subsumed. As soon as the Chinese encroached upon the steppe, they were forced to adapt to the terrain and its climate. They became different from each other and no longer conformed to the norm. The Chinese could not dwell at "the marches of the world" without losing their status as human beings.[24] The concept of a well-defined

Groom. Detail of a terra-cotta statuette of the Tang dynasty

Above and overleaf: Brick wall at Jiaoshan, in Hebei Province. 41

東丹避詡主越
海芎秦彥侶作
射鹿圖慢胡獵
舊裝改姓事他
圖回心悵故鄉
雜年亟歷志熟
雲出未忘達妮
吳太伯近稿澤
高皇
乙酉仲秋月
再題

The Stag Hunt. Painting by Huang Zongdao, ca. 1120

and rigidly fixed frontier was inherent in the political and cultural principles of Chinese civilization, and the Great Wall was the expression of this concept. But in practice, such an inflexible concept could never be applied completely. So despite all the sacrifices made on its behalf, the Great Wall never constituted anything more than an approximate frontier.

THE XIONGNU ORIGINALLY lived in the northern part of what is now the province of Shaanxi. When the Qin and Zhao states expanded westward in the fifth and fourth centuries B.C.E., they were expelled to the steppes, where they constituted a powerful confederation of tribes from the third century onward. Most historians consider the emergence of this threat to be one of the reasons why the first emperor of China decided to exclude them. Whether this was the cause or the consequence, there will always be a question mark over the original relationship between the Great Wall and the barbarians. Chinese tradition is unequivocal on the subject, however. Li Po, one of the great classical poets, put it succinctly:

In the past the Great Wall was built to fix the habitation of the barbarians
Subsequently, towers with flaming torches were constructed.[25]

Tumen was the first Xiongnu khan driven from the Ordos by Qin Shi Huangdi when the sections of the Great Wall were linked (at the end of the third century B.C.E.). His son, Modun (209–174), is considered to be the first great ruler of this nomadic people. Sima Qian is again the source for the few events that are known in the lives of Tumen and Modun. He apparently based his information on an epic saga that was circulating by word of mouth among the wandering peoples of the time (see page 52).

Barely a century after the building of Qin's Great Wall, Modun had a series of confrontations with emperors of the new dynasty of the western Han. In 198 B.C.E. a peace treaty and alliance was concluded between the Xiongnu and the Chinese. The Han emperor officially recognized the sovereignty of his neighbors over the northern territories and frontiers of China. In return, Modun recognized the sovereignty of the emperor of China over the lands beyond the Great Wall. It is on the basis of these historic barters that the Chinese image of the barbarian was formed.

Modun, Son of Tumen
209-174 B.C.E.

Y ou have made us powerful and bloodthirsty, O Son of Heaven! You have pushed us back beyond the land of our ancestors. By your will, we have become outlaws. Better still! In order to ensure our banishment from the world, you erected a wall. Do you know that at the same time you created an enemy who would threaten your borders for centuries to come? And that you introduced a fear of strangers into your hearts that would last for thousands of years?

Remember! We had common ancestors. We became the Rong or Ti nations, already defined as barbarians, living on the fringes of the kingdoms of the north. In the mountains, the forests, or the swamps, we kept ourselves apart from the peoples of the plains. We were more familiar with wolves, foxes, tigers, and other wild beasts than with priests and worship. We were different in every way—what we drank, what we ate, what we wore. We could not exchange civilities; our languages did not permit us to understand each other. At the same time, enfeebled and dispersed through the valleys and hills, we barely survived the rigors of winter, attacks by wild beasts, and the Qin wars.

Our territory of the Ordos is a hostile one, a world of barren soil and steppe. Our ancestors, who were neither sedentary farmers nor nomadic shepherds, did not know the fertility of the Wei Valley or the flowering of the civilization that developed there. The best that the hardiest among us could hope for was to place himself in the service of Qin and, in accompanying him on his conquests, discover the magnificence of the neighboring kingdoms.

Must I recall that we owe our freedom to the first emperor, the unifier of China, to the walls built by Qin and Zhao? We did not want to be forced to till the soil or contribute to the prestige of the empire. So he drove us out and condemned us to the worst punishment that he could conceive—he gave us our freedom. The "ferocious beast" turned us into the people of the steppe. In this immense, open, and hostile world, having become nomads and shepherds of the wide open spaces, we drew on new strengths. We preferred our chanting and our war-drums to your poems sung to the accompaniment of the cithera. We created a sanctuary for ourselves out of the great expanses of our exile. Unconquerable, we leapt upon you, the sedentary ones who think you are

Preceding pages: Tartar horsemen

protected by your wall. Emerging onto the scene on our swift horses, we harassed your retreating guards and your disoriented horsemen with our arrows.

In order to civilize yourselves, you created barbarity! Like the savage spirals of wind and sand that beat against your ramparts, you see us full of cruelty and cunning. We are made in the image of our deserts and our plateaus, austere and grandiose. How different from the fragile and precious beauty of your craftsmen! Look, Son of Heaven, see how the implacable law of life inspires our goldsmiths and our blacksmiths. Even the outlaws of your empire who bring their skills to us are converted to our lordly impulses. Using our bronze and our gold, they have cast a tiger pouncing on a hart, the contortions of bodies in violent attack and confrontation, fighting to the death. Everywhere the image of the beast, natural and unforgiving, prevails, or is re-created in imaginary combinations. For we love to wear the symbols and magic of the hunt on our belt buckles, our votive offerings, and on the tops of our standards. Whether wolves or panthers, rams or roebuck, carnivorous beasts of the mountains and forests, hidden in the thickets, these representations of animals with slavering jaws and crushing limbs are the manifestation of our "barbaric" art. A cruel art, you say? As cruel as our fate.

This has been the rule of my life. As he became aware of my ambitions, Tumen, my sovereign and father, removed me from power. As soon as I reached adolescence, he left me in the hands of our neighbors to the west, the Yueshe, who avoided showing their hostility only as long as they were estimating our strength. Tumen launched a surprise attack upon them, in the hope that they would kill their hostage. But I foiled all of their ruses and escaped on their handsomest stallion. I returned to my own people, to be feted like a hero by them.

After this trial of strength, you will understand, you who reign unchallenged, that my greatest victory was to banish any faltering of my determination.

This feat won me the command of ten thousand horsemen. I turned them into an implacable fighting force that would bring me to supreme power. My will had to be accomplished at a single sign of command. I trained my troops by leading them in the hunt. As soon as I shot a whistling

Turkoman horsemen

arrow at the prey, all of them had to imitate me without a hint of hesitation. That is how I began, by taking the lives of those who were most afraid. Then one day, as we were training our stallions, I identified my favorite horse as the target. Not everyone responded to the whistling arrow. I exterminated the cowards.

But there were still too many question marks. Shortly thereafter, having noticed one of my favorite wives, I dispatched the fateful arrow straight to her heart. All that I now needed to do was to show how I would proceed. I shot a whistling arrow into the troop of horses owned by my father, the sovereign, aiming to hit his favorite mount. I had the satisfaction of seeing myself obeyed in every respect. The time had come to act. Shortly thereafter, while I was out hunting with my father, I shot the death signal at him. The multitude of arrows that hit him made it impossible to distinguish mine from all the rest, thus marking the end of his reign through collective sacrifice.

Thus did I gain power over my own people through their submission and their fear.

All that remained to be accomplished was to unite the steppe and subjugate the neighboring tribes. The lands to the east, beyond the passes, were the territory of the Donghu tribes. They took it into their heads to ask me for my best horse, famous far and wide for its beauty and strength, an *argamak,* the swiftest racehorse. Against the advice of my lieutenants, I decided to accede to their request. Emboldened by what they considered to be my timidity, the Donghu then asked me for one of my favorite wives. I gave her to them, again despite the disapproval of my advisers. Finally, the Donghu demanded an expanse of our pastures that they coveted. I asked my counselors for advice. Most of them replied: "Offer them this territory! In any case, what does our opinion matter? Yours is the only decision that counts!" Then I exploded with rage. "How can one concede land, the root of a nation!" I put my evil counselors to death and immediately launched my horsemen against the Donghu.

They were taken by surprise, conquered in a single battle, and I made them into submissive subjects. Without wasting time, I turned my new forces against the Yueshe tribes in the west. They fled frightened, panicked, and weakened beyond the deserts before I could turn the skull of their king into a drinking cup. I had no rivals. Since then, I have reigned over the empire of the steppe.

Ever since, sovereign of the Han, here we are face to face, rivals linked by the wall that covers thousands of *lis,* as much an unexpected bond as an accursed barrier. Through your implacable will you wanted to unify the nation and impose harmony upon it. Within well-defined limits, you encircled the great mass of your conforming and submissive subjects inside a wall. You excluded land that was not suitable for farming and individuals that failed to conform to the norm. It was easier to seize the Ordos than to submit us to you. So rejoice at seeing us flee from your benevolence and favors! Do not reproach us for pillaging your granaries and coveting your riches! Your wall is our salvation. It would be the end of us if, having scaled it, we found ourselves cut off at the passes. Your cities and even your villages would be so many shackles for us, places of perdition that would ruin our soldiers and destroy our courage. Our victory would merely precede our enslavement.

I was delighted to learn that you do not want to conquer us. You quite rightly fear sending your armies into the uncharted, arid steppe. This would be beyond your abilities, and such a campaign would threaten the stability of your empire. I now accept your offerings, these rolls of silk and jars of wine, these bushels of grain and other foods. Receive in return cattle, woolens, and furs. I appreciate your wisdom without being duped by your gesture. Today the relationship is "peaceful and friendly,"[26] tomorrow it will be war again. At the point where our empires meet, our rivalries do the same. The wall is inadequate protection for your power. You will still need to reassure yourself of the loyalty of the guardians of your frontiers. If you pressure them too much into obeying, they will be tempted by the freedom of my wide, open spaces. I have welcomed more than one of them who was fleeing from your might. I have more than one name to whisper to you. There is that of Han Xin, or the king of Qibei, or the king of Huainan. You may well fear that those of your people who venture too far into the steppe will become one with it, drunk on the expanse, and that they will join me.

Your wall does not separate our two worlds. It is the axis along which our influences mix and combine. It covers a marginal land in which our whole lives combine without destroying one another. There are repercussions, in your empire as in mine, of the effects of a hybrid culture upon our daily lives. There is danger in such a mixture! It is a permanent struggle to avoid the complete assimilation of one into the other![27]

O f the long list of despotic rulers that have governed China, some were greater builders of walls than others. Each of them did so in his own way, and this explains the diversity as well as the extent of the fortifications, the expression of diverse policies in relation to the northern and northeastern frontiers.

Wudi ruled the Western Han empire from 140 through 87 B.C.E. His was the dynasty that succeeded that of the first emperor. From the very start of his reign, a period of prosperity, Wudi's ambition was to subjugate the Xiongnu. To this end, he sought alliances with other barbarians in the western territories. He opened up the road to Turkestan, first by researching the territory, then by extending the Great Wall right to the limits of the deserts. This policy would have definitive effects on China's expansion into central Asia.

In the north, Wudi restored or reinforced the wall that Qin had built and added another line of fortifications to it, south of the existing ones. In 138 B.C.E. he sent an emissary named Zhang Qian into the remote western world to propose an alliance to the rulers of the lands bordering the Celestial Mountains, so as to surround the Xiongnu in a pincer movement. Neither the king of Tayuan

THE HAN WALL AND THE WESTWARD EXPANSION

Earthen wall of the Han period, Shandan region of Gansu
Turkish or Mongolian hunter. Painting from the Southern Song dynasty

Terra-cotta horse of the Tang dynasty
Earthen wall of the Ming period, near Qingtongxia Zhan in Ningxia Province

Bronze horses and chariots, Eastern Han period
Preceding pages: Flock of sheep returning home near Zhenbeipu 71

Kazakh hunter with his trained eagle, Bayan-Ölgi, Mongolia

The Great Wall at Mutianyu, north of Beijing

(Ferghana[28]) nor the king of Taxia (Bactria[29]) was won over by the proposal made by the emperor of China; during his twelve-year voyage, however, Zhang Qian discovered that the peoples of distant lands bred magnificent horses, and these were needed by his sovereign in order to fight the Xiongnu.

The Wusun were a pastoral nation who bred their horses in the valley of the Ili,[30] between Lake Balkash and the Tian Shan[31] range. The wealthiest of them had as many as four or five thousand horses. They were thoroughbreds, of the type still bred by the Kazakhs in the valley of the river Tekes, a tributary of the Ili. The king of the Wusun sent a thousand of them as a wedding gift for a Chinese princess promised in marriage by the Han imperial court.

The fastest mounts were those of the land of Tayuan (or Tawan, in Ferghana). Zhang Qian described them as "sweating blood,"[32] and of good size, the result of crossbreeding with wild stallions in the mountains. Their attributes won them the title of *tianma*, "celestial horses." Apparently it was the Parthians who originally created the breed, believed to be the oldest in the world, in the fourth century B.C.E. The Turkomans have jealously preserved it to the present day under the name Akhal-Teke.

The reports brought back by Zhang Qian caused Emperor Wudi to decide to send his armies out to conquer the Hexi (now Gansu) Corridor, which was under the control of the Xiongnu, so as to be able to put his trading relationship with central Asia on a firm footing.

The brave leaders of the campaign were warlords who had been singled out from the masses for their talents as horsemen. Two colorful leaders with outstanding personalities led this heroic struggle. Wei Qing was responsible for the first victories over the Xiongnu in 127 B.C.E., and his nephew Huo Qubing completed the conquest of the Hexi in 121 B.C.E. The latter is famous for the very popular story of how, after a victory, he poured a jar of wine sent by the emperor into the basin of a stream so that all the soldiers would have a chance to taste it. Hence the name of the city of Jiuquan ("Source of Wine"), and its promotion to the status of commandery—as was the case of Wuwei.

To protect Gansu, which consists of a long series of oases between the Mongolian plateau and the high mountains of Tibet, the Great Wall was extended from Lingju (in what is now the district of Yongdeng[33]) to northwest of Dunhuang. At this location, a fortress was built with the evocative name of Yumenguan, "the Jade Gate," the reference being to the jade brought by caravans from the Kingdom of Khotan[34] (Hetian) in the southern Taklamakan Desert.

At this point, the Great Wall was not built for strictly defensive purposes. On the contrary, it was one of the elements in a resolutely offensive strategy of advancing toward the lands of the west. Beyond what is now Xinjiang, watchtowers and fortresses were erected to protect the first stages of the road leading to Turkestan and onward right to the very shores of the Mediterranean, the Silk Road. In that direction, the Great Wall and its extensions of fortified garrisons right up to the Pamir Mountains represented the outstretched arm of Chinese imperial power extending toward the limits of the known world.

The history of the Great Wall is accompanied by the inseparable, haunting, and vital story of the quest for the best horses. That is why whenever the empire was at its strongest, it implemented a complex policy of relations with central Asia, involving trade, strategic marriages, awards of honors, and alliances against a common enemy. Thus what was Silk Road in one direction was Horse Road in the other, leading to an indispensable supply of cavalry mounts.

In ancient China the horse had been used in warfare to draw war chariots. The use of warhorses was first witnessed on the battlefield in the eighth century B.C.E. in western Asia and was adopted in China around the third century B.C.E., in Qin, which lay close to the lands of the northern barbarians. The rulers of China, whose land was mainly used for cultivation, had no good bloodstock, and the peasant population were poor horsemen, so they had to seek both horses and riders from among their enemies in the north or among the peoples of the west.

The statuary found around the tomb of the first emperor is evidence of this borrowing from the peoples of the steppes, who served as examples and as enemies. Originally, the great ritual sacrifices made by Chinese sovereigns consisted of bulls, sheep, and pigs, while the worthiest offering of the nomad was the horse. The steeds used by Qin and at the start of the Han dynasty were apparently identical to those used by the Xiongnu, and resembled the modern small Mongolian horse, a sturdy, thick-necked breed. It is a significant indication of the interaction and exchanges that when, in 49 B.C.E., a treaty was concluded on the banks of the river Orkhon (Orgon) between the emissaries of Xuandi, emperor of China, and Huhanye, Chanyu of the Xiongnu, a white horse was immolated and his blood mixed with the wine drunk by the signatories.

Emperor Wudi initiated trading with the kingdoms of central Asia from 114 B.C.E. Every year, a dozen caravans of about a hundred men left China, loaded with silk, precious metals, jade, and corals, which they would trade for horses.

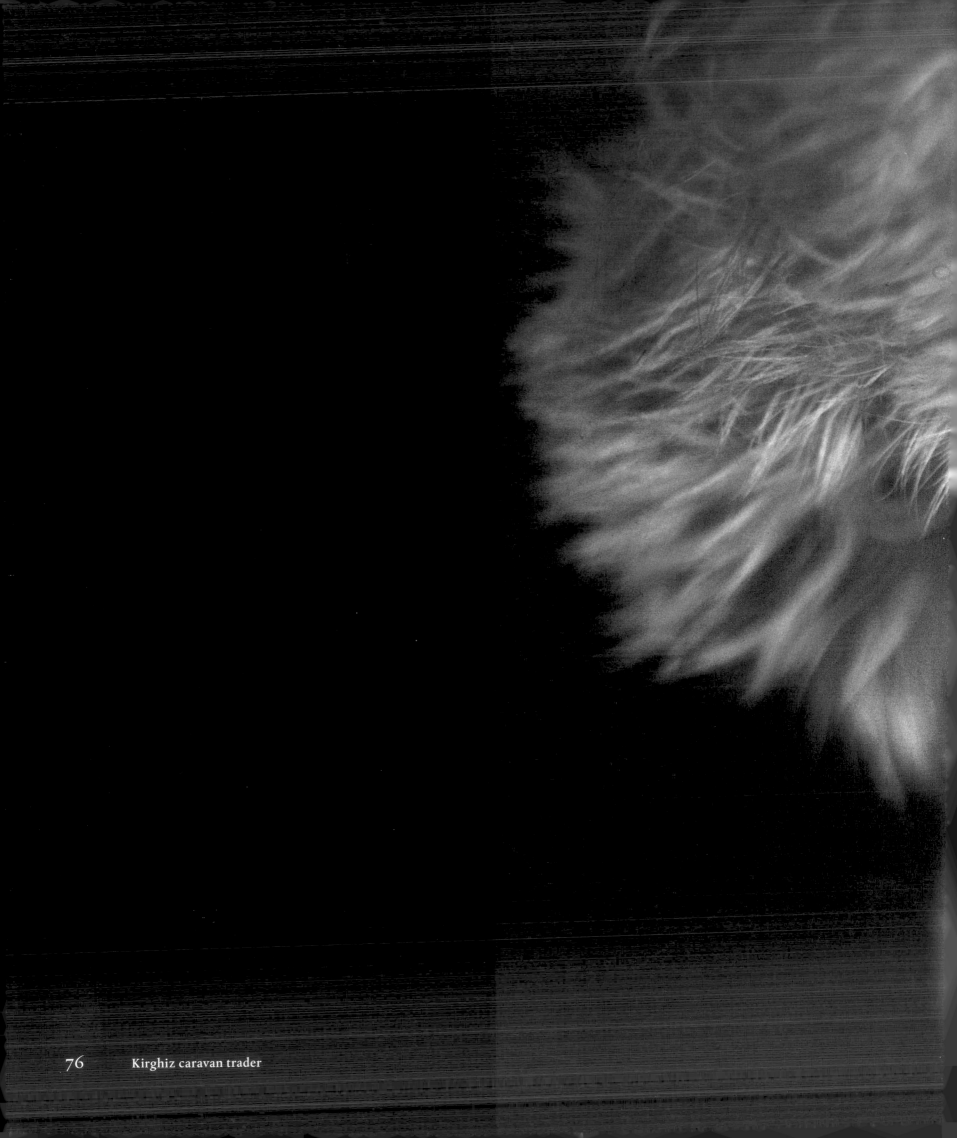

Kirghiz caravan trader

The inhabitants of Tayuan grew tired of these incessant requests, eventually rejecting the gold coins of the imperial emissaries, whom they then proceeded to massacre. Outraged, but still in great need of the "celestial" horses, Emperor Wudi sent a first punitive expedition against Tayuan in 104 B.C.E. It failed disastrously. A second expedition of 60,000 men returned after four years of bitter fighting and huge losses with 20 or so magnificent horses and about 3,000 stallions and mares of lesser quality, though many perished even before reaching China. Whether they were an imperial whim or a strategic option, a high, even exorbitant price had been paid for these horses, one that took no account of the hardship or loss of lives of human beings.

Near Chang'an (now Xi'an), ancient capital of the Western Han, a statue representing a "naked horse dominating a Xiongnu barbarian" stands at the foot of the burial mound of Huo Qubing, a brave cavalry general and a great horseman. This monument, testimony to the valiant deeds of a hero who died at the age of twenty-four, whom Emperor Wudi wanted to have buried in a tomb near the one he was building for himself, is an expression of the period. It was rediscovered in 1914 by Victor Segalen, who produced a scholarly and poetic description of it. He saw it as "the result of a doubly Chinese art,"

though without denying the other influences that might have guided the sculptor's chisel. He recognized in the busy composition, arranged to give the feeling of power, the distinctive Mongolian pony of northern China, the double of the one he rode on a daily basis. He expanded his vision before this statue so that it encompassed the open plains on which the Han Chinese and the barbarians confronted each other in battle. "Other more enduring monuments lie here beneath the impalpable matter, stories and poetry that have undergone little change, and that transmit the elegance, civilities, and spiritual joys of the time. It would be fair to include the emperor himself among the great poets. 'Here is the flower and the perfume, a perfume more alive than the flower; a flower more solid than the walls around the garden that produced it.' Today the Great Wall is being buried and is submerged, but the lines of Han Wudi are revived again each spring in the hearts of the scholars. Yet in order for them to germinate, another wall was needed, one that separated poet and barbarian, a fiery, living wall beyond the Great Wall, whose towers and redoubts were the sturdy infantry and the advance camps of the squadrons of Huo Qiuping [Qubing]. This statue remains the rigid symbol of the conflict, one that we have inherited."[35]

In the seventh century the Tang dynasty regained a foothold in central Asia, and because they were closer to the barbarians, they were intensely involved in the world of the steppe and the horse. Of all the gifts arriving from the western regions, the horse was the most eagerly anticipated. Horses are depicted among the clay funerary objects of the period. They have a small head, a wide forehead, protruding eyes, a long, narrow, straight nose, wide nostrils, a sharp, elongated lower jaw, a fine, arched neck, an elegant body with a shiny coat, long tapering legs, and a long mane and tail, the latter attached high on the supple body.[36] Li Shemin, the true founder of the dynasty under his imperial name of Taizong, was an enthusiastic horseman, to such an extent that he surrounded his tomb with bas-reliefs showing "six famous racers" from the imperial stables. Pottery featuring polo players engaged in a frenetic game are evidence of the popularity of the sport at the Tang court. The imperial stables contained as many as 600,000 or 700,000 horses, an incredibly large number, indicating that the cavalry had the resources to launch waves of mounted fighting men well beyond the Great Wall, or what remained of it. The defeat at Talas[37] in 751 against the Arabs was the start of the withdrawal of the Tang to their traditional farmlands and the peasants who had no room for horses.

Emperor Yongle of the Ming dynasty wanted to maintain a cavalry corps to be used in his offensives against the Mongols. To this end, he organized tea trading in exchange for horses. This arrangement had originally been set up by the Northern Song (960–1127), who held markets along the northwest frontier. Tea was popular with the barbarians. It was easy to transport, healthy to drink, and warming after long exposure to the cold. The imperial power granted a monopoly to the "tea-horse bureau" (chama si).

The tea came mainly from Sichuan and Shaanxi, and the bureau traded it at its outposts at Hami, Koukou Nor, and Dunhuang. The cost of maintaining and feeding several thousand horses and men was ruinous, especially in the region of the steppes, and the arrangement of trading tea for horses did not bring the hoped-for results. It was probably considerations of cost that made Yongle decide to gradually withdraw his remotest garrisons, those stationed between the wall and the Gansu Corridor. This still left the knotty problem of finding an adequate supply of horses. In the late fifteenth century the court traded bolts of silk for horses and Bactrian camels, depending upon the quality of the animals offered.

Portrait of an officer and a horse. Terra-cotta figures of the Tang period
Overleaf: The Ming Wall at Mutianyu

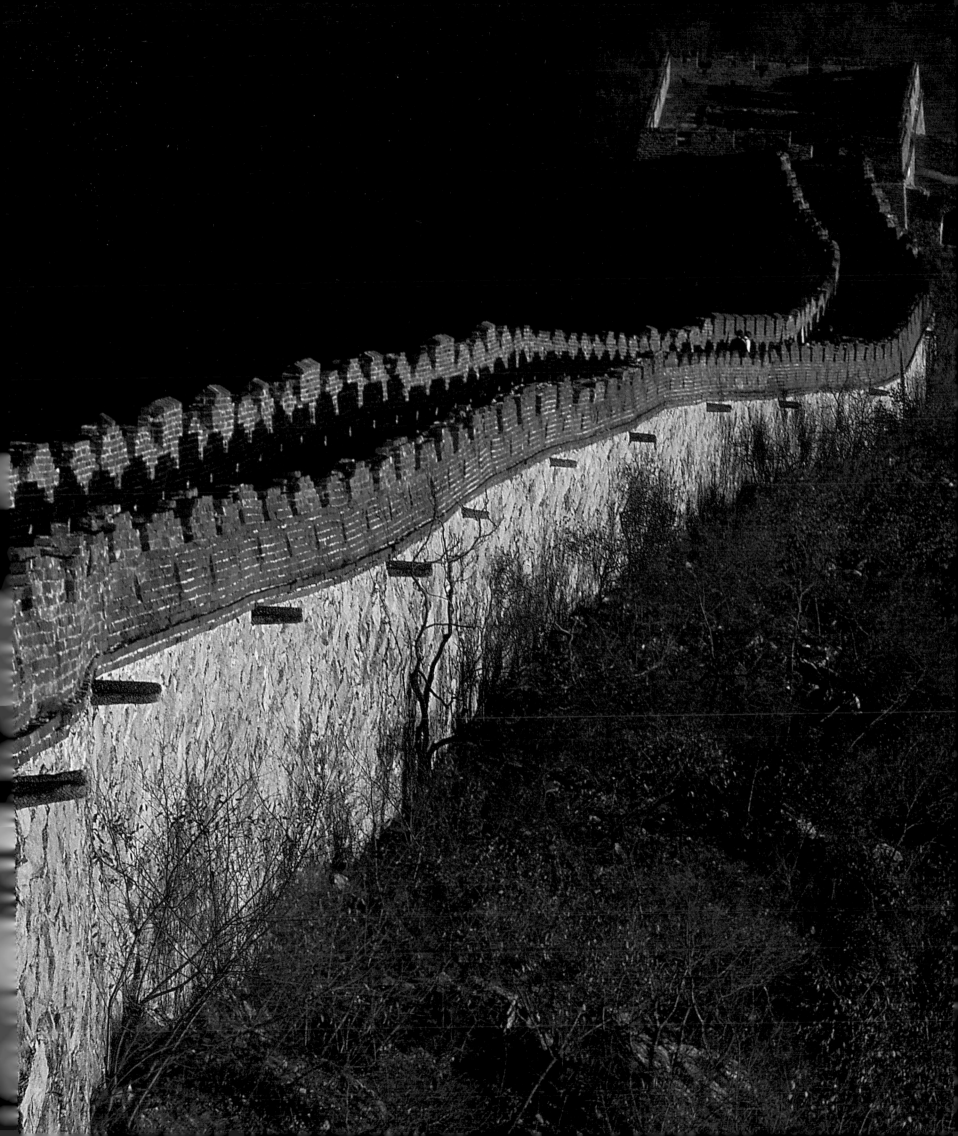

Buddhist monk
The Sangim River and the Buddhist caves of Bezeklik, near Turfan

It was always difficult and costly for the empire to control the caravan routes along the distant western borders and maintain garrisons along and beyond the Great Wall. Trade with central Asia ended when the Han lost the Tarim Basin,[38] between 23 and 74 C.E. and after 127. Its temporary reconquest by Pan Zhao under the Eastern Han (first and second century C.E.) was another odyssey that even led to direct contact with the Roman Empire. It was not until the second century C.E., according to the most recent research, that Buddhism, Indian influence, and the Greco-Buddhist art of Gandhara reached China by this land route, as a result of trading links.

The ancient Jade Gate, in the far west of Gansu, beyond Dunhuang, opens onto the desert. When the north wind raises a moving screen of dust, it causes the line of towers that punctuate the ruins of the wall to disappear. Such places, in which everything is death and desolation, would surpass others at eliminating distractions, and there are so many reminders of those who passed this way centuries previously. In such a place of solitude, it is easy to perceive the meaning of each vestige of the distant past, in the days when this frontier post at the edge of the desert was permanently occupied. The bastions of the wall became a refuge for those who guarded it, for those who had to endure arctic temperatures for half the year and suffocating heat for the rest.

Buddhist monk on a pilgrimage. Tenth-century painting on silk

IN ADDITION TO MARVELING at the folly of the enterprise, the whim of a despotic ruler, there is the amazing fact that here the wall still stands, as solid and almost vertical as ever. What is striking is the skill of the military engineers and builders who erected it, the way in which they used the topography to their advantage in siting the bastions and ramparts, doing so with the utmost efficiency and economy. At this point, the line follows the relief of the landscape, leading to a terrace on which a watchtower has been built over a dry riverbed. It then turns northward to run beside a swamp, a natural ally in defending a right of way. Signaling towers have been sited every half-mile or mile along the line of the foothills. In such an arid environment it could not have been easy to find suitable materials or water. Yet these structures, built of alternating courses of earth, branches, or reeds, have resisted the constant assaults of the forces of erosion for more than two millennia.

The wind of the past blows through a crenellation in the wall or over the top of a watchtower. This is particularly true in winter, when the visitor huddles into an angle of the wall for protection against the icy blasts sweeping in from Mongolia. Names scrawled on a brick are yet another time line, signs of a life lived long ago, desperate imprints on a gigantic levee. The imagination tries to impose a shadow on this stage set of stone and compacted mud. The shades of the long-departed are watching, guarding, and controlling the pass.

We are aided in our quest by the ancient ruins, covering hundreds of miles beside the route of the Great Wall, that are evidence of the daily lives covering a period of two millennia and the destinies of the builders, soldiers, messengers, and travelers by caravan at the outermost reaches of the empire. It is a most moving experience to discover traces of the passage, a sort of scent, a mark that has not been obliterated despite the centuries that have since passed, of the patrols that guarded the wall.[39] Arrowheads, bamboo tablets inscribed with characters, shreds of tethers, sometimes even a clothes bag still bearing the name of the owner, a scrap of shantung silk, medical prescriptions, edifying reading matter or simple handwriting manuals, tools and utensils, in the form of piles of debris or mere fragments, express the toil of this humanity chained to and sacrificed to this monumental barrier.

I imagine two people meeting in this desolate landscape whose emptiness is so propitious for making such discoveries. The first of them is Sir Aurel Stein, the great archaeologist and early twentieth century explorer, who reconstructed with brilliant perception what life must have been like in the early Han garrison at the wall beside the Jade Gate.

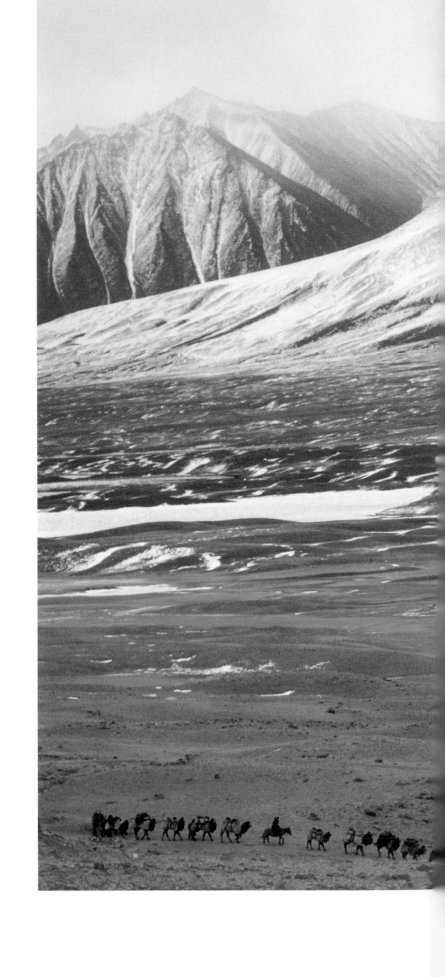

Bactrian camel. Terra-cotta of the Sui period
Above and overleaf: Kirghiz caravan on the roof of the world

89

Bactrian camels. Terra-cotta figures from the Tang dynasty.

The view enjoyed from the top was
    wide and impressive.
To the south, I could see the scrubby depression
    merging in a belt
of Togrbak and tamarisk jungle.
Beyond there rose an absolutely bare gravel glacis
towards the equally barren foot hills of a great
range far away. To the North-East four towers lit
up by the sun behind us could be made out
echeloned in the distance, silent guardians of a
wall line which I thought I could still recognize
here and there in faint streaks of brown shown up
by my glasses. What a fine position, I thought,
this height of the fort wall must have been for a
commandant to survey his line of watch-stations,
and to look out for the signals they might send
along it.[40]

More than two thousand years ago, *the*
commander of the Linghu company, one of
the companies that manned the barrier during
the Han dynasty, contemplated the same
expanses, though with very different feelings,
affected by a long, enforced exile and
the threatening presence of the barbarians
close by.

Brick wall in the Huanghuacheng region, north of Beijing
Winter landscape. Fifteenth-century Turkish-Mongolian miniature

The Commander of the Linghu Company
c. first century C.E.

The barbarians are back! A small group of horsemen appeared suddenly on an outcrop and have been watching us. The threat to the empire is never far away, but we have never felt it to be so close. Since this alert, we have been preoccupied with worry. My men are asking themselves how the next battle will go. Flags and pennants have been raised on the watchtowers. We are the Linghu company, known as "destroyers of the barbarians," a title that says a lot about our alleged courage! Yet, where would we be without the virtue of our sovereign, we, the soldiers of the confines and farmers at the gates of the desert?

It happened at the end of the day. It is the time when people remember how they left their village and the faces of their loved ones, when everything melts into the last colors and the first shadows. I was gazing southward, seeking to discern the blurred stain of the oasis. In the distance, above a strangely thin low cloud cover, the line of snowy peaks stretched out of view. It was as luminous as a pale shroud beneath the setting sun. My spirit flew to she who is embroidering a poem for me. But none of those white clouds is ever in her image.

The sound of the watchman's horn suddenly broke the silence. That sinister sound, so unexpected since it had not been heard for so long, lingered as if it were trying to flow back and wake the entire ten thousand *lis* of the Great Wall. Until that moment, the threat of the barbarians seemed to have been eradicated. They had vanished into the northern desert, as if fleeing the appeasing benefits of civilization.

Despite the surrounding calm, our orders remained perfectly clear. We were to watch for any signal transmitted from tower to tower from the distant garrisons of the west, lost on the shores of the Lobnor or, farther still, right up to Luntai,[41] at the foot of the Celestial Mountains. We had witnessed the passage, on more than one occasion, of hundreds of soldiers from every region of China, most of them reprieved from the executioner, making for the desert. They were off to establish *juntian*, military colonies living on newly cleared agricultural land, bringing their families with them in an exile from which there would be no return.

We are also here to prevent the outlaws of the empire from running away from it. Whether they are mere deserters, bandits fleeing their crimes, or princes disobeying orders from the capital, all intend to join the ranks of the barbarians and threaten the empire from that land without roots. But I have also seen large bands of starving peasants fleeing from the poverty of the cruel regions of Hexi, staring hallucinated at the steppes, imagining that they will find a more bearable fate there than the hell they left behind.

Occasionally, we welcome caravans that arrive from distant kingdoms whose people have strange customs. It takes them weeks to cross this sea of sand, reaching Lobnor[42] after following the Kunlun Mountains, or the recently opened northern route, leading directly from the Celestial Mountains. After inspecting the list of what they are carrying, we create a specific inventory of the presents they are offering and their merchandise. We assure ourselves that these strangers will be capable of respecting our customs, and we often need to teach them how to behave correctly.

More than once, I have had to remind my incredulous soldiers that to protect our empire effectively, we needed to turn our backs on the steppe and survey the interior. "How is it," questions the most daring of them, "that the threat does not come from the barbarians? What would happen if they crossed the barrier?" I have needed to use my powers of persuasion and proof of vigilance to convince them that the unity of the empire is paramount. It is not significant if a single troop of barbarians manages to cross the Great Wall at one of its weak points. It is far more important to be sure that a single mode of thinking will predominate, indivisibly, within the passes and that no one should try to distance themselves from it, keeping the entire nation united in harmony.

In the capital, a partial forgetting of the barbarians had caused the frontier garrisons to be consigned to oblivion. The wind, the cold, the burning sun, and sometimes the rain continued their relentless and indefatigable work of eroding the fortifications. In certain places, the depradations were so great that the wall had become a mere mound of earth. In others, where it had been built of stone, peasants from the neighboring villages had misappropriated the boulders for building homes.

That is why the call of the watchman, issued like a cry of fright, made me turn, stupefied, to watch the expanses of gravel running northward to the horizon. In these vast arid stretches, laid out like huge scales, the biting wind has carved the rock strata into sharp blades. One rarely sees human beings emerging from this hostile and menacing world, let alone faces. The few wild beasts that are seen assume that there is a primitive and cruel world out there. The void of these inhospitable lands is intolerable to the human mind. We feel most deeply anguished when the east wind brings a warm breath of spring, laden with the fragrances of farmland, to our arid plains.

It was at that very time of year that I saw, on the crest of a hill, the outlines of men dressed in skins and bristling with weapons.

They were terrifying, welded to their mounts in a way that made them look like monsters. Their immobility exasperated us and emphasized our disquiet, since this was their way of letting us know—and with what contempt!—of their next incursion. The watchman had drawn his crossbow and shot an arrow in their direction. They disappeared into their petrified world as suddenly as they had appeared. Riding over the grayness of the nearest stretches of sand, all that remained between us was the long line of bare hills that blocked the northern horizon in a fantastic and chaotic series of peaks, cliffs, and rocky slopes, without a trace of vegetation, whose color scheme ranges from pale brown to dark purple.

This apparition put an end to the torpor and silence in which we were wrapped. Tired of waiting for my impossible return to my homeland, I had tried to dismiss the memory of the fields that surrounded my town and the current flowing in the Great River.[43] To escape from boredom, for months I had taken refuge in routine tasks, such as accepting and storing wheat brought from the Dunhuang oasis, writing an order to deliver clothing to the guards, building a storeroom, and other occupations required by this outpost of the empire. I do not know if the commander of the Jade Gate misunderstands my zeal. Separated from my loved ones for years, I hide my pain behind a mask of impassivity.

Having been sent on a distant campaign, I have submitted to my bitter fate and have devoted myself to everyday toil, such as building up rows of brick to reinforce the barrier, collecting and carrying fuel to light the beacon fires, and maintaining the mud huts that are our only shelter.

What was seen yesterday was followed by another strange sight. A violent north wind suddenly arose, as often happens in this season, and caused a fire to blaze up that had not been properly extinguished. This was due to the negligence of my men, but forgetting their own carelessness, they immediately associated the phenomenon with the sight of the barbarian horsemen and interpreted it as a sign and portent of a major incident. The flames spread to the brush and reeds beside a swamp and thence to the groves of tamarisk and wild poplar. As night fell, a blanket with living, red fringes was devouring the land that it was our duty to protect. The poplars caught fire and exploded in a shower of sparks. They illuminated the interior of the wall, as if to better demonstrate its vulnerability.

At first light, I went over to the burned-out shore that combined the strange proximity of water and fire. Close to the water's edge, I tried to avoid the marshy ground by making numerous detours. At the very moment when the soil became firmer at the edge of the depression, I had to

Preceding pages: Loess landscape in Shaanxi

pick my way around clumps of brushwood that was still glowing. The abundant white efflorescence of salt on the earth contrasted strikingly with the blackened poplars and tamarisks, as if two forces faced each other in battle, as a prelude to new encounters along the frontier.

At dawn, a horseman came from the Dunhuang command post with a message. In a few days' time, the governor would be arriving to inspect the barrier. It was time to assemble the members of my company and fill the gaps left by deserters.

Along the frontiers, there are many forts but few men. The governor would be accompanied by the inevitable band of officials, scrupulously cutting costs at the expense of others, and more dangerous than the barbarians. They would calculate on wooden tablets the daily allocations of bushels of wheat, black linen for the soldiers' clothing, payments of silver for the lower ranks, and would count the number of days each man had been serving at the frontier.

Every ten *lis*, the watchers would man the towers. They would show their swords, their Henan shields, and especially their powerful longbows and crossbows, and the quivers containing one hundred and fifty regulation bronze headed arrows. Every five *lis*, a whip would be raised high to order the cavalry to mount. Horsemen patrolled along the barrier. They made tracks in the great sandy desert while waiting for the Huns to assemble.

It is ten days since we saw the barbarians. The news from other points along the frontier is alarming. One company's camp was ransacked and set on fire. Two hundred of our men were wiped out. Jiuquan was besieged, but snowflakes began to fall as the first assaults began so that a fire could not be lit to make smoke signals. Farther to the east, near the river that had already frozen over and was hard as a rock, they swore to sweep away the barbarians, even at the expense of their own lives. Three thousand men dressed in skins perished in the sands. Piles of anonymous bones are heaped on the shores. Still, when spring comes, their wives will dream of them as men.

A serious attack is expected. The chariots and horsemen are on the alert. At night, signaling by beating on his pot, the watchman counts the hours in the sand and the darkness. When the wind blows, one thinks one hears the sound of the *piba*, mixed with sobbing. The wild geese, flying invisibly over our heads, accompany their flight with plaintive calls.

As dawn breaks, we climb the heights to watch for the smoke of the alarm signals. A light hoarfrost covers the sand and outlines the outcrops. Our banners clatter in the wind, though the wading bird in the nearby marsh is undisturbed. But when the drums resound and the trumpets blare, it is frightened and flies away. That is when the battle begins.[44]

The Ming Wall at Jinshanling, near the Gubeikou Pass 103

Earthen wall at Bataicun, Shanxi Province

Armed with lances and protected by their
    breastplates,

Shaft against shaft and crossed blades.

The standards hid the sun, faced with waves
    of enemies,

Under a rain of arrows, the warriors rivaled
    each other in ardor.

Our ranks have been smashed, our lines broken;

The horse on my left has been killed, that
    on my right is wounded.

Both wheels are jammed, the four horses
    immobilized,

I seize the drumsticks and beat the drum.

Heaven is against us, the spirits are full of rage;

Warriors exterminated to a man, bodies
    scattered over the plain,

They have come and will not go back, gone
    without returning,

Into indifferent spaces, along distant roads,

Carrying long swords, and bows seized
    from Qin.

Behind them, decapitated bodies, whose
    hearts remain unvanquished.

They were full of courage, and ready to continue
    to fight,

Determined to the end, irreproachable.

Lifeless bodies, spirits without breath,

Phantoms of the souls, they have become the
    genies of the brave.[45]

Woman playing a *wude*. Terra-cotta figure of the Northern Qi dynasty

Earthen wall at Bataicun, Shanxi Province

THE TANG DYNASTY AND LIFE ON THE FRONTIER

The Tang founded their dynasty in 618. They extended their power to central Asia, well beyond the walls built by their predecessors, of whom the last were the Sui (581–618). The policy of expansion into central Asia involved the armies in long campaigns against the western Turks west of the Tian Shan range. For the many and talented poets of the period, the Great Wall and its locations, especially the Jade Gate in the western marches of China, became the most evocative symbols for the classic themes of separation, war, and death. Separation and distance from nearest and dearest became even more unbearable beyond the wall. Although it was rarely mentioned, the name of a famous pass was symbolic of the enforced separation, the break between the two worlds. The fact that the official religion lacked mystical tendencies and expectations intensified

Ladies of the court. Terra-cotta figurines of the Tang dynasty
Winter on the Ming Wall at Jinshanling

the anguish. Meditation went no further than contemplating the vanity of material things, and the wall in particular. A typical Chinese poet lived in the lowland plains, and respected the social order and agriculture. He was peace-loving to the core. If he was ever moved to glorify sacrifice and conquest, he seemed to be more inspired and more sincere in evoking the passage of time, the exhaustion and suffering of service on the ramparts, watching for signals from the top of a tower, and love of his sweetheart from whom he had been separated for so many terrible months and years.

In this respect, Wang Wei (701–761) has become the symbol of this period, which combined poetry and the plastic arts to their best advantage.[46] One of his short poems takes us from the capital city to the distant lands beyond the Jade Gate, the very edge of civilization:

At Weicheng[47] the morning rain wets the fine dust,
Beside the inn, the willows are turning green.
Empty another glass of wine!
Once across the Yang Pass [48]
You will find yourself friendless.[49]

This period witnessed exceptional interaction between China and central Asia. The Tang dynasty established a general protectorate called Anxi, "the Pacified West," beyond Gansu. Its "four garrisons" were located at Kucha, Sule (Kashgar), Khotan, and Karashar.[50] For those who had been exiled beyond the wall, and who longed for home, this meant that the welcoming lands had moved closer. The Luntai fortification in northern Tarim, founded by the Han, was revived under the Tang. A governor and a colony of soldier-plowmen maintained this point at which caravans could take on fresh supplies.[51] Cen Shen (715–770), a scholar sent to the western confines of the empire, is the great poet of the frontier. On the occasion of the departure for home of his friend "Secretary Wu," he describes the harsh climate and desolate expanses:

The north wind sweeps the land, the white grass
*   snaps.*
Under the sun of the Hu barbarians, it snows after
*   the eighth moon,*
One might believe that in one night, a sudden
*   spring wind*
Caused a thousand and one pear-trees to blossom.
Snow penetrates through the pearl curtains and
*   soaks the silk hangings.*
Neither fox fur nor silk comforter can keep us
*   warm.*
The general holds his horn bow with difficulty,
And the governor finds it hard to wear his cold
*   armor.*
A thousand feet of a sea of ice covers the desert to
*   the horizon*
And sad, dark clouds are immobile for ten
*   thousand lis.*
The military secretary invites us to drink wine on
*   your departure,*
To the sound of lutes, citharas, and barbarian
*   flutes.*
Before the camp gate, the evening snow falls
*   heavily,*
The wind no longer makes the frost-stiffened red
*   banners flutter;*
I accompany you to the Eastern Gate of Luntai,
The Road to the Celestial Mountains is all white.
When you have turned the corner of the road
*   and disappeared,*
Only your horse's hoofprints will mark the snow.[52]

The founders of the Tang dynasty had barbarian blood in their veins, and their expedi-
tionary force included Turkish cavalry units.
Many of the governors and administrators of the
western regions were of central Asian origin. It
was their job to maintain peace and security on
the frontier of the empire and to collect tributes.
Caravans traveled the length of the Hexi (Gansu)
wall, bringing back Tang horses, camels, sheep,
eagles and falcons, leopard skins and sable furs,
jade, precious stones, golden vessels and coins,
and woolen fabrics, all of which were destined for
the court. The game of polo was introduced at
court. In exchange, Chinese technical know-
how—weaving, papermaking, and printing—was
exported westward, spreading from Kocho[53] to
Samarkand and even as far as Baghdad. The Tang
poets celebrated the renowned music and dance
of Kucha, but they lamented the price paid for it—
the endless watch for the warning dust clouds,
"the bones of the warriors buried every year in
the desert" so that bunches of grapes from Kocho
(near Turfan) could reach China.

Encampment on the Mongolian steppe

The Great Wall in spring at Huanghuacheng   115

THE MOST BEAUTIFUL AND complete expression of the Chinese soul is through poetry, and it is all the better if it is accompanied by painting and calligraphy, arts that were widely practiced from the fourteenth century onward. For those better at expressing their emotions than at analyzing them, the poem excels at creating an atmosphere. The Great Wall is too concrete an object and is thus a poor source of inspiration, but everything it evokes and all those feelings and images that it arouses—exile, separation, distance, war, and death—feature in a multitude of works of art. The same themes persist over the centuries and the dynasties—the lament of the soldier, the dreary landscapes of the steppe, guarding the northern frontiers, the misery of the abandoned wife, wars in distant

territories. In short, all those unhappy facets of human existence have been sources of inspiration, transformed by the power of the imagination into literary masterpieces. The wall, the barrier, the mountain passes, all had a painful fascination for the artist, arousing and capturing his emotions.

Women feature prominently in the symbolism of this poetry. Whether wife or courtesan, she translates or expresses loyalty, betrayal, sadness, courage, or resignation.

She is often the victim, sent against her will "outside the passes" *(guanwai)*, inevitably to a strange and barbaric land, to be given in marriage to seal an alliance, a practice common during the Han dynasty. In their new and distant home, the exiled princesses were the most fragile and pathetic witnesses to their strange world. A short poem has made one of them famous. She was Sikiun, daughter of a minor member of the royal family from central China. She was offered to the king of the Wusun, who were apparently the Alain, a tribe of blond, blue-eyed nomads who inhabited the western slopes of the Tian Shan, and with whom the Han emperor Wu had concluded an alliance against the Xiongnu. In the fall, during the last days of warm weather preceding the rigors of the central Asian winter, and when the migrating birds fly away to China, Sikiun expresses her deep sadness:

To the world's end I was married.
My Lord is the King of Wusun.
To his strange tents I was carried
With fleeces their walls are hung.
Only mutton for food, and the milk of mares!
I long for my father's kingdom night and day.
Endless my exile, useless my tears.
O for the wings of a bird to fly far away! [54]

On the other hand, the beauty of a courtesan can cause a sovereign to lose everything, cause the downfall of his empire and the triumph of the barbarians. One of the favorites of the Han emperor Wu (140–87) was celebrated by her brother, Li Yannian:

In the north there is a beauty who is so lovely,
That no one else looks beautiful beside her.
With one look she can raze ramparts to the
     ground,
And with a second look the kingdom is defeated.
Who knows whether, once walls and kingdoms
     have fallen,
The beauty's pride will be restored? [55]

If certain Chinese authors are to be believed, the end of a dynasty, accompanied by barbarian incursions, was also an opportunity for regeneration, thanks to the contributions from outside, and this might explain the longevity of Chinese civilization. The Great Wall and its defenses were incapable of keeping the warlike and insolent nomads at bay, and these marauders were thus able to establish themselves on Chinese soil, raiding frontier villages and towns at will.

At the end of the Han dynasty, *around the year 200, the daughter of Cai Yong*, a fashionable court poet and scholar, was abducted during a Xiongnu incursion. The captive Cai Yan has left as a legacy one of the greatest poems by a woman, "Eighteen Verses Sung to the Hun Cornet." It is full of spontaneous emotion and untrameled by literary convention. The Great Wall lies at the heart of this evocation, a derisory defense incapable of protecting an empire under siege and preventing the collapse of a decaying society. But it is also the dividing line between the fate of two worlds (see page 120).[56]

Polo player. Terra-cotta of the Tang dynasty
The Great Wall at Mutianyu

Cai Yan, Daughter of Cai Yong
200 C.E.

My early life was unclouded, until misfortune visited my country. The pitiless heavens have since rained down troubles upon me that the equally pitiless land has forced me to endure. The iron weapons clashed and the roads were barred as we tried to flee from suffering and death. Smoke and dust obscured the fields as the barbarian soldiers led their captives away. The rule of law and justice disappeared, reason tottered. Lost forever as I am in this hostile world, who will hear my plea?

Alone, abducted by these hordes unleashed, I am forced to follow them to the ends of the earth. The way back is cut off from me by cloud-topped peaks.

There are spirals of sand everywhere, raised by the desert winds. The cruel and ferocious barbarians, with their arrogant airs, parade in armor with their crossbows at the ready in their hands.

Torn from my beautiful country, China, I am no longer anything in a city of tents in the midst of the barbarians. The walls and clothing are of felt and wool. The most disgusting experience is having to eat their stinking mutton. All night, until daybreak, the drum sounds are accompanied by the hideous howling of the wind that sweeps over the plain and obscures the camp and the mountain passes.

Day and night, I am haunted by the memory of my native soil, I am the unhappiest creature on earth. The angry heavens have sown discord and turned the people away from their master. I am lost forever, captive in the barbarian camp, where everything is foreign to me, so how can I continue to live? Alone and friendless, who can understand my pain?

I should like the ducks that fly south to know the sounds of our frontiers. When they return northward, I believe I hear the sounds of my homeland. But they fly so high that one can barely see them passing. I suffer and tremble, but my homesickness does not grow less.

Hoarfrost and ice cover the plain. The bitter cold brings me new suffering. Despite my hunger, I cannot eat their cheese. The torrent of floodwaters disturbs the night, and in the morning, beside the wall, the paths are flooded. I dream of a past that is gone forever.

After sunset and in the mournful whistling of the wind the barbarians everywhere become noisier. I have no one in whom to confide my sufferings.

In the mournful desert where solitude reigns, the bonfire beacons extend into infinity. This world is implacable for the weak and the old; there is no salvation for those who are bereft of strength and youth. The fields and streams of the borderland have nothing in common with the land of my birth. Cattle and sheep cover the plain in innumerable herds. But once the water has dried up and the grass has been eaten, the sheep and cattle graze elsewhere.

Will the ruling heavens look down upon the earth to release me from my miserable plight? How can the wise and powerful spirits leave me in this distant exile? Why has heaven given me a barbarian for a husband? What harm have I done to the spirits to be treated thus? The sky is infinite and the earth is endless, and the pain in my heart is boundless and nothing can alleviate it.

Life is brief, as fleeting as the dawn. Destiny has not permitted happiness to illuminate my fate. The sovereign heavens, that have willed the loss of my youth, remain blue and deep, inaccessible to my pleas. In the void over my head, there are only clouds.

> The beacons of the Great Wall will never be extinguished.
> Peace will never reign over the battlefields.
> The spirit of murder floods into the passes every day, like a wave.
> And every evening, under the moon, the wind howls and fills the space.

Although I have no fear of death, I am not avid for life, yet I cannot renounce it as long as a spark remains. The hope of one day seeing my own country again keeps me alive. And if I die and am buried here, all will be finished forever.

O stars in the heavens! Beneath the tents of the barbarians, one of them married me, and I brought two sons into the world, I care for them and feed them without remorse. Although they were born in the northern deserts, I love them. We are united forever, they are my flesh and blood.

A spring wind blows from the east. It is so warm! It is the emperor of China bringing sunshine and peace to the world. The barbarians leap about and sing with enthusiasm when they learn that the war is over between China and themselves. But here is the Chinese envoy, who has come with a thousand ounces of silver to ransom me from the barbarians.

124

126   Turkoman women in their yurt, Afghan Turkestan

The Great Wall at Huanghuacheng

130   Terraces under cultivation at the foot of the Great Wall, north of Beijing

132   Young Kazakh musician, Mongolia

THE LEGEND OF MENG JIANGNU that is directly connected with the Great Wall is known to all Chinese, even the most illiterate, in various forms. The oldest text dates from the Springs and Autumns period, the Zuochuan. The first version, as moving as it is revealing, is that of a wife faithful to the memory of her husband, without any reference to a wall. It is not until the Tang dynasty (618–906) that Meng Jiangnu is faced with the tyranny and cruelty of the first emperor.

As winter approaches, the heroine tries to find out how her husband is faring, since he has been deported by a scholar to help build the Great Wall. She finally reaches the building site after a long journey and learns of the death of her husband, so she breaks down sobbing. Her tears cause the wall to crumble, and the remains of her husband appear so that she is able to give him a decent burial, as befits a widow in the Confucian tradition.

After the Tang period, the legend of Meng Jiangnu continued to be popularized in various forms, in stories, poetry, novels, plays, and paintings. Under the Ming, an additional element was added to the story in that the drama unfolds in the Shanhaiguan (Shanhai Pass). The myth having become a reality, the tomb of the heroine and the temple (built by the Ming) dedicated to her can be visited near this section of the Great Wall, though no wall existed at this point in the time of the first emperor, when Meng Jiangnu is supposed to have lived. Even today, in its most popular form of street theater, the performance of the legend of Meng Jiangnu, a heartfelt expression of Chinese culture, defies every modernizing trend, since it takes place against the backdrop of the Great Wall, the monument to suffering.

Detail of a fifteenth-century Turkish-Mongolian miniature
The Great Wall at Simatai

Bas-reliefs in the "Cloud Terrace" in the Juyongguan (Juyong Pass)

Preceding pages: The Great Wall at Heituo Shan, north of Beijing

On the eve of the Mongol invasion, in the early thirteenth century, the Toungous, who were sinicized but remained brave fighters of the Jin dynasty (1115–1234), ruled a vast territory covering Manchuria and a large part of northern China. To protect themselves in the west from their Mongolian neighbors, they built earthworks preceded by ditches over impressive distances. There were two main walls, one extending to the foothills of the Da Hing'an Ling[57] range, a distance of about 300 miles (484 km), and the other from the meander of the Yellow River to the Soungari River plain, a distance of more than 1,000 miles (1,600 km). Other lines of natural protection, the Yan Shan and Taihang Shan ranges, which could only be crossed through passes, had always been defended against invaders. Finally, in the plain, more cities were protected behind the barriers of high fortifications, right up to the Shandong Peninsula.

Genghis Khan launched a campaign against the Jin kingdom in northern China in 1211. It was fought over territory that was new to the Mongolians, since they were used to the steppes, oases, and scattered populations. Farmland, villages, and cities had a building density that made them slow and hard to besiege and destroy. There were also

GENGHIS KHAN AGAINST THE JIN KINGDOM

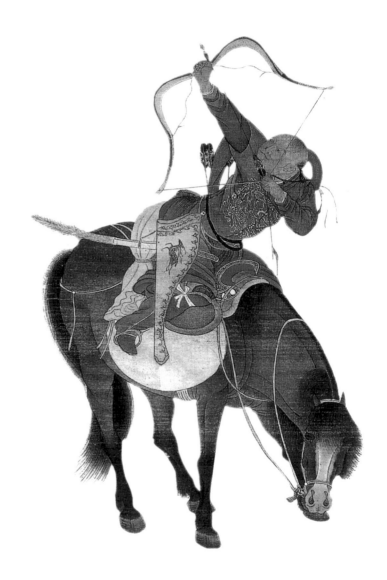

The Great Wall at Heituo Shan, north of Beijing
Detail of a painting of the Yuan period

too many inhabitants to be killed or deported. In short, the murderous hordes threatened to become bogged down:

We horsemen know nothing of sowing and reaping.
But any land that can be plowed and whose
grassland can be ridden,
We have covered.

We do not deign to build walls or temples,
But any town that can be burned with its walls
and temples,
We have burned.

We carefully honor our wives who are all of very
high rank.
But the rest who can be overcome, abducted,
and taken,
We have taken.

Our seal is a spearhead; our festive clothing is
armor where the dew crystallizes;
Our silk is woven horsehair. The other, softer kind
that is saleable,
We have sold.

Frontierless, and sometimes nameless, we do not
reign, we travel.
But everything that can be cut and split, all that
can be nailed and shared . . .
In other words, whatever can be done at the point
of a saber,
We have done.[58]

In order to reach Beijing, home of the Jin court, Genghis Khan had to cross the Juyong Pass, northwest of the capital. The pass was summarily fortified because the wall that now lies across Badaling was not built until 350 years later, under the Ming. According to Chinese tradition, Genghis Khan managed to get through, using a trick to circumvent the pass. The *Secret History of the Mongols* explains how the Mongols employed their classic maneuver that consisted of fleeing in order to lure their attackers into pursuing them, so they could turn upon them:

. . . In the year of the Sheep [1211], the **emperor Cinggis launched a campaign against northern China. . . .**

He sent two men in advance, Arrow and Buzzard.

Arriving at the Gulley [Juyongguan], since the Gulley neck was well fortified,

Arrow said: "We shall provoke them, force them to move, and draw them here; then we shall put them to the test!" And he turned round. Seeing them turn back, the Chinese troops said to themselves, "Let us pursue them!" and they set off in hot pursuit [in such great numbers] that they covered mountains and valleys.

Upon reaching the spur of Hsüan-te fu, Arrow turned around again and launched himself at a gallop at the enemy, who were arriving in scattered ranks. The emperor Cinggis, with the bulk of the army, attacked those he had left in his wake. . . .

Arrow captured the gate of the Gulley, captured the narrows, and passed through them.[59]

The Mongols and the Yuan emperors had no reason to maintain the old fortifications or build new ones. Their empire now included Chinese and barbarians on either side of the walls that had been erected by previous dynasties. They merely built a few palaces and pagodas in the Juyong Pass for the use of the emperor, should he honor them with a visit. All that remains of these structures is the "Cloud Terrace" (*yuntai*), an imposing stone mass embellished with handsome Buddhist sculptures.

Lassoing a horse, twentieth-century Mongolia

Overleaf: The Great Wall at Jinshanling 145

THE GREAT WALL
OF THE MING

The Ming dynasty (1368–1644) has left contrasting traces in history. At the risk of oversimplification, the period can be summarized by two images. The first is the sea voyages to distant lands led by Admiral Zheng He, a eunuch, who took his ships as far afield as East Africa, a unique exploit in Chinese history. The second is the image of the impressive sections of wall of stone and brick, crenellated and festooned with bastions and towers, constructed in the last decades of the dynasty (but especially in the sixteenth and early seventeenth centuries C.E.).

When it finally liberated itself from Mongol domination, China inherited from the Yuan the remains of an empire that was wide open, extending beyond the traditional territory of the sedentary population. The energy and even brutality of the first Ming emperors did not prevent them from preemptively sowing the seeds of the forthcoming decline, by fostering the exclusivity of the imperial clan and the rivalries between the scholars and the eunuchs. The Forbidden City was home to a succession of "sons of heaven," surrounded by courtesans and ladies of the palace. This confined world gradually succumbed to the influence of the south. It was there that the scholars, with their narrowly nationalistic views, defenders of the

Detail of a painting of the Ming period
The Great Wall near the Huanghuacheng reservoir, north of Beijing

150   Detail of a painting of the Yuan period

Ramparts at Pingyao, Shanxi Province   151

"civilized" world and opposed to any compromise with the barbarians of the north, had sought refuge in the "rural academies."

The achievements of the Ming dynasty are notable in an ambiguity inherent even in the name, which means "clarity" or "light," a light that is more blinding than illuminating. The founder, Hongwu (1368–1399), was the troublesome chieftain of a band of brigands of a sect known as the White Lotus before becoming emperor, when he turned Confucian and conservative. His was the idea of incarcerating the members of the dynasty behind massive walls of his new capital, Nanking, and his birthplace, Fengyang,[60] while retaining Peking (Beijing) as the northern capital.

After swiftly expelling the Mongols, the previous rulers, he seems to have been overcome by the expanse of space in the north, though he apparently did not want to commit himself to it entirely. The intermediate world between China and Mongolia had no established borders, apart from the traces of constructions erected in vain by previous rulers. Hongwu thus began his own search for a frontier. Unlike the Tang, he had no affinities with the barbarians and did not dare to embark upon an overtly aggressive strategy. In establishing a line of eight fortresses, he laid the foundations for a wall that would be built a century and a half later. The bastions and signal towers, rebuilt from the ruins abandoned by the Yuan or erected from scratch, sustained the mobile units of troops who operated as a vanguard in sorties against the Mongols. These structures remained modest, however, consisting of small earthworks that fell easy prey to the ravages of time.

TWO SMALL FORTS, MARKING each end of the fortifications, were built at this time. The ancient Jade Gate of the Han, at the extreme western frontier on the edge of the desert, was abandoned in 1372, in favor of Jiayuguan, almost two hundred miles eastward. The narrow passage that opened the route to central Asia had been borrowed by the Chinese colonies first established during the conquest of Turkestan. The eroded terrain is dotted with bare peaks and deep ravines. Nothing has changed for centuries, and time slips by without trace, like the clouds from the distant Pacific Ocean that occasionally waft across the sky. The void and silence are accomplices in the terrible trap that changes wonderment to anguish, an anguish that befell the men and women marching into exile to a land "where no poplar grows, where no spring wind ever blows." How many survived to see the hoped-for day when they could once more enter "within the wall," while forever remembering the words of farewell laden with eternity that were engraved on their hearts?

If you turn to dust at the frontier passes,
I shall be the rock at the top of the mountain![61]

Civil servant of the Qing dynasty
Overleaf: A winter's day at the Imperial Palace   153

Hanging Palace of the Green Cliff

Young Han girl, Autonomous Region of Ningxia   157

At the other eastern extremity, "on the seaward mountainside," the Elm Pass (Yuguan) opened onto the road to the great northeastern expanses. It had always been necessary to contain the nomadic or sedentary nations of the area, the Nuzhen, the Toungous, and the Manchus, tempted by the riches of the southern plains. "Gongs are beaten, and drums played in the Elm Pass; and the banners snake across the Standing Stone Mountain." Just north of this passage, but still on the coastal plain, Hongwu built another defense, the first at Shanhaiguan, the "Pass between Mountain and Sea."

Yongle, the third Ming emperor, was a man of the north, a magnificent sovereign who maintained the ambiguous nature of the dynasty despite being a usurper. Throughout his reign, he took time to supervise the construction of impressive walls erected around Beijing, the city he had made into his capital. He intended to chase the Mongols away forever and personally headed five expeditions into the heart of Mongolia. But shortly thereafter, for reasons that the historians have failed to explain adequately, several of the frontline garrisons that had been the geographical bases for the steppe campaign were abandoned. This enabled the Mongols to gain control of the marches and gave them access to the Ordos.

The elements were thus assembled for a drama in several acts, leading to a tragic ending. They consisted of the capital, the most spectacular defenses of the Great Wall summarily sketched in by Hongwu in 1368, and the Yan Mountains, antechamber to the barbarian wastes.

First there was the bustling capital city, in which the eunuchs had gradually gained dominance at the expense of the scholars; it was the center of a civilized, orderly world. As emperors came and went, the apparently carefree life of Beijing masked a growing number of intrigues and political maneuverings relating to the policy adopted in relation to the nomads. The scholars had at first taken refuge as far as possible from the court, but their spirit of unrest reached the capital. Careers were ruined and perpetrators condemned, but nothing and nobody escaped the pitiless demands of the frontiers, involving separation, sacrifice, and death. As if to create a stepping-stone into the unknown universe, Yongle chose a magnificent site in a valley north of the capital for the imperial tombs. The tumuli surrounded by walls and enclosed by pine thickets have their backs to the mountains, not far from the wall that defends them against the invading hordes.

The uniform and intensely cultivated plain abuts brusquely against the high reliefs of the Yan

Shan range. The ridges of the peaks are rough and sharp, and the passes are narrow. The scholar sent as a government official to the frontier confronted this other world and looked back, "his saber at his side, his hands clasped, gazing longingly toward the capital,"[62] in a final salute to those he had left behind. He abandoned the spring, the peach blossom, and the shade of the willow trees to enter a world of snow and cold, where the wild geese flew overhead as nostalgic links to those he had abandoned. Generations of exiles have used the same allegories to express their sadness or despair as they trekked northward.

Up to this point there was no wall worthy of the name. The Ming began to build their first ramparts south of the Ordos from the late fifteenth century, creating the frontier walls (*bianqiang*) where the "Nine Frontier Garrisons" (Jiu Bianzhen) would be posted. But they thought it unworthy or unfitting to combine their defenses with the Great Wall (Changcheng) built by the first emperor, Qin Shi Huangdi, that lay farther to the north.

And in the north, there were the barbarians! They had never gone away, and they returned in force in the early fifteenth century, fanning out across the northern borders. The Toungous, who occupied the northeastern fringe close to Siberia, had been conquered by the Ming in 1368. The Nuzhen, who occupied eastern Manchuria, had been split apart by the Ming, who cunningly exploited their tribal rivalries, but now they began migrating southward from Korea to the eastern frontiers of the Mongolian plateau, eventually encountering the Chinese frontier garrisons. To the west, the Mongols were becoming ever more daring and constantly harassed the Chinese on the frontiers.

EVEN IN THE FACE OF THE Mongol incursions that threatened the whole empire, the court was paralyzed by clan warfare. Those who favored engaging in hostilities and launching expeditions in reprisal were opposed by those who favored negotiations and trade with their turbulent neighbor. There was nothing new in the way this overrefinement sat cheek-by-jowl with savagery. It was a situation that had endured for centuries, maintained by pulsations as brutal as they were disconcerting.

From the fifteenth century onward, Ming policy was largely responsible for fueling the acts of aggression committed by the Mongols in Chinese territory. The main reason was the refusal of the Ming to trade with the Mongols, who then took by force that which they had been prevented

The Yellow River in Shanxi

The Yellow River and the Great Canal, detail of Ming map
Overleaf: Rapids on the Yellow River at Hu Kou, Shanxi

from acquiring by fair means. Mongol aggression was curbed by terrible periods of long drought of a type frequent in these regions or by their need to wage war on rival clans, especially the western Mongols.

The Ming government's refusal to trade was not for economic reasons. Today, it would be interpreted as ideological, based as it was on the traditional Chinese attitude to the outside world. This thorny question had been tackled many times, and different answers were given, depending on the period. In the second half of the second century B.C.E. the Han had adopted a policy of disguised tolerance or "peaceful and friendly relations," *heqin,* that involved exchanging tributes and marrying Han princesses to the barbarians. Subsequent dynasties—the Northern Zhou, the Sui, and the Tang—had adopted similar principles and acted accordingly.

There were also those who were so hidebound, trapped by their hairsplitting and haughty concept of hierarchy and correct relations between nations, that they ruled out any contact between civilization and barbarity, between China and the barbarians, *hua* and *yi.* For centuries the point of reference was the lively and shrewd debate between the scholar and statesman Jia Yi (201–160) and the Han emperor Wen:

The Xiongnu are no more numerous than the population of a large Chinese district. The fact that a great empire fell beneath the yoke of a mere district is something that should be a source of shame for those who are in charge of the affairs of the empire. . . . The situation in which the empire finds itself could be described as that of a person who hangs his head. The Son of Heaven leads the empire. Why? Because he must remain at the top. The barbarians are at the foot of the empire. Why? Because they should be placed at the very bottom. At present, the Xiongnu are arrogant and insolent, while they invade us and pillage from us, showing how disrespectful they are of us. The damage they have done to the empire is infinite. Despite all this, every year, the Han Chinese bring them money and silk. Rule over the barbarians is a power that has been granted to the emperor who is placed at the top, and offering tribute to the Son of Heaven is a ritual which the vassals that are at the very bottom should observe. It is incomprehensible that the situation should be reversed.[63]

While sterile arguments continued in the capital city, the Mongols managed to unite under the leadership of one of their number named Yexian (Essen). The concentration of their forces and newfound daring enabled them to inflict a crushing defeat on the Ming forces in 1449, when they captured the emperor at Tumu, on the north shore of

Lake Guanting, which can be seen from Badaling, less than sixty miles from Beijing. This event resulted in placing the Ming irretrievably on the defensive, even though they were still unable to adopt a definitive political strategy.

The main question, the crux of the argument from the mid-fifteenth through the sixteenth century, was the situation in the Ordos, the meander of the Yellow River that had become grazing land for the Mongolian herds and a departure point for their sorties against Chinese territory. Those who favored leading an expedition against the nomads and rejecting any diplomatic and commercial contact continued to prevail at court. They were supported by the educated people, more of whom were becoming converted to the philosophical ideas of the scholars of the south. According to their uncompromising stand, it made no sense to enter into a relationship with the barbarians, and peace would mean humiliation for China. Their narrow definition of patriotism caused them to brand their opponents as traitors.

Those who favored a more conciliatory policy were mainly officials who had direct experience of the Mongols. They advocated a combination of measures, especially the development of trade, to control and stabilize the situation on the frontier. Attempts at conquest seemed to them as pointless as they were dangerous for the army, expensive for the state coffers, and destabilizing for the population.

A portrait gallery of stereotypes has survived from this long period of feuding between moderates and diehards. There were patriotic heroes, such as Xia Yan (1482–1548), executed on imperial orders as the culmination of a long series of struggles for influence, and cruel and ambitious traitors such as Yan Song (1480–1565), his rival, the high secretary, who was in favor with Emperor Jiajing. It was the emperor's personality that contributed to the closed world of intrigues and rivalries during his reign. As a native of the south, he hated the barbarians so much that he required the character *yi*, which represented the word "barbarian," always to be written very small! He preferred worship of the spirits to affairs of state and organized Taoist religious ceremonies in search of eternity.[64] Intrigues and quarrels, executions at court, and unrest along the border continued for about a century and a half. They resulted in a single compromise—the erection of walls, with a period of frenzied construction that lasted from 1567 through 1620.

Han peasant in Shanxi
The Great Wall at Mutianyu   169

Peach trees in blossom at Hebei

Preceding pages: Loess landscape in Shanxi

The Great Wall at Jiumenkou, between the provinces of Hebei and Liaoning   173

Refusing to trade with the Mongols and incapable of vanquishing them on the battlefield, the Ming could find only one solution, namely to lock the nomads out of their world by building walls. This was not the result of a considered policy, or even of a cultural consensus. It was the outcome of dissension that within a few decades would lead to the gradual collapse of the dynasty, a kind of suicidal defeat, organized by a divided ruling class.

ALMOST ALL THE STRUCTURES that continue to fire the imagination are the product of only half a century of rejection and isolation. They maintain the myth of the "Great Wall measuring ten thousand *li*," the work of the first emperor at the dawn of the Empire.

Throughout the first Ming period, architects and engineers building the wall were inspired by the same techniques as those that had been used by their remote predecessors. The walls built south of the Ordos after 1474 were still earthworks, ramparts destroyed by erosion in a matter of decades. The French paleontologist and philosopher Teilhard de Chardin, who traveled through the region in the fall of 1923, described the ravages of time as follows: "Leaving Mongolia for a week, we pushed eastward in an exploratory trip into China itself. For us, entering China meant crossing the Great Wall. But at the point at which we crossed it, the old rampart had been almost completely destroyed and covered by drifting sands. Yet from *li* to *li*, the towers that marked the line of wall remained proudly erect, and to right and left, as far as the horizon, their diminishing outlines could be discerned hugging the mountains that edge the Mongolian steppe to the east and south."

The first walls built in the Ordos in the early fifteenth century encouraged the Mongols to gradually advance east of the Yellow River, toward the complex, mountainous terrain that separates the Mongolian plateau from the great plain of northern China. Passing through the walls meant taking routes that were controlled by the Taiyuan, Datong, and Xuanfu[65] garrisons. These new migrations by the Mongols were accompanied by acts of aggression and caused the Chinese to decide to reinforce the major passes that led to Beijing, by extending the wall. Faced with these new obstacles, the Mongols used a detour that led them northeastward and eastward.

In the sixteenth century, the military defenses created north of Beijing, from Datong through Shanhaiguan, became more elaborate. The frontier garrisons were reinforced, and new concepts and techniques were used for building the walls. So from 1572 bricks and stones began to be used in the Datong region, to replace the earthworks, for all of the walls, towers, and other fortifications.

In less than two centuries, the Ming had constructed the elements of the *bianqiang,* the "frontier wall" from the far end of the Gansu Corridor to the Yalu River in Korea. Whether of earth or of stone, it represented the most imposing defenses ever built.

The line of defense north of the capital, erected mainly around the second half of the sixteenth century, remained the most spectacular and complete. The guard towers, watchtowers, crenellated walls with arrow slits, flights of steps, and bastions protecting the gates become part of the landscape, following the crests of the mountains or blocking the passes. The main citadels, located at strategic points, which still fire the imagination, convey a false impression of invulnerability and continuity. Although these recently restored sites exist only at the far ends of the line of fortifications and close to the capital, they are sufficient to restore the illusion that the solid wall really extends for ten thousand *lis,* and that they constitute a summary of its history.

AT THE WESTERN EXTREMITY, "the yellow sand rises to the white clouds and the lonely wall melts into the impressive mountain."[66] The image was a powerful one for the ambassadors who came from central Asia, emerging from the long trek over the desert and reaching the Gansu Corridor as one would reach a distant shore. The first outpost of the empire, the sovereign sign of the Chinese world, was to be found amid the sand and gravel. One of the ambassadors sent to the court of Emperor Yongle, between 1419 and 1422, by Shah Rukh, "son of the terrible Tamerlane and one of the greatest sovereigns in Asia,"[67] brought back the first evidence from an outside witness. "On the following day [August 27, 1420] they marched across the desert. When they reached a fortification called Karaul, in a mountain pass, through the middle of which the road passed, the whole group was counted and their names recorded before they were allowed to continue on their way."[68]

From 1495, and for about a century, the citadel was erected, taking the shape that it retains today. The main elements were built of brick, and to protect the approaches, earthen embankments were added to the Han earthworks. Jiayuguan is an unexpected or improbable sight in an unforgiving environment, an architecture that is elegant despite its purpose. The powerful heavy mass of the gates and ramparts supports pavilions whose roofs have upturned flying corners. The fortress, implanted in the dry climate with its extremes of cold and heat, is the best-preserved complex of Ming buildings. The high walls with their crenellated parapets, the gatehouse towers and the angle-towers, take one back in time to the Middle Ages or to the Orient as depicted in sketches made by the voyagers of old. Three vaulted gates that echo to the sound of footsteps precede the little camp hidden behind these ramparts. Jiayuguan is a staging post on the Silk Road, an image pasted onto the desert, a cliché in Oriental style.

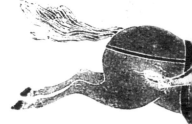

Hanging Palace of the Green Cliff
Statuette of a man, terra-cotta figurine of the Western Han dynasty

FAR FROM THIS ATMOSPHERE of neglect and solitude that confers such majesty on Jiayuguan, the Juyongguan (Juyong Pass), less than thirty miles (48 km) from Beijing, has unfortunately been turned into a sort of amusement park in recent years. This is where the Ming emperors erected their first buildings ca. 1368, reinforcing them after the Battle of Tumu, before completing the whole complex in the sixteenth century. Since it is so close to the capital, the wall at Badaling, north of the pass, hosts a continual stream of visitors from every continent. The site has been cheapened and submerged, and is now a mere caricature of the "Great Wall ten thousand *lis* long." This representation of a dream or heritage from a great era is now drowned in hideous, frenzied, raucous commercialism. More grandiose or more grotesque developments of the site are promised, depending on the mentality of the celestial bureaucrats.

Gubeikou, farther to the east, is the "ancient northern pass," worth a visit to contemplate the fall colors, especially in the light of the setting sun. A bastion perched on an escarpment of the Yan Shan range dominates the river Chao. It is difficult to realize that this quiet place, dripping with heavy humidity in the summer, was ever

of strategic importance. The road to Chengde attracts a few customers, tempted by the hideous greasy-spoon eateries that disfigure the landscape. The pass had a historic role to play in the grand story of the Great Wall, but today it is harder to see past the present structures to its natural beauty.

Continuing eastward, along the sections stretching from Jinshanling to the edges of Simatai, the sights become more impressive. Once the hordes of tourists have disappeared, the naked walls and the hills behind them exert an obvious charm in the silence. The kind of solitude that is an impossibility at Badaling opens up perspectives of time, so that one's mind dwells on the intensive labor and the deep ravine. The sharp peak of Simatai, topped with crenellations, indicates a prowess that was as insane as it was useless. Here the stone monument, anchored into the rock, is like a line of sea foam, frozen in an ocean of crested waves. There is no question that for its guardians, the Great Wall was all-embracing

Preceding pages: The Great Wall, near Huanghuacheng

and devouring, a place to wait for war but without the hope of returning spring.

Continuing on to the sea, the obsessive exclusion line ends at Shanhaiguan, the "Pass between Mountain and Sea." At this point, however, it was not the Mongols but the Manchus who were watching out for the weaknesses of the empire. From the late fifteenth century through 1584, imposing fortifications were built to serve as a barrier across the coastal plain, replacing the initial modest encampment. A citadel was created, preceded by a curtain wall in which there were gates under vaulted roofs, and flanked with more walls that continued right into the sea. The pavilion that dominates the main road still bears the proud inscription, "The first gate under heaven" (*Tianxia diyi guan*).

Shanhaiguan features in the suicidal end of the Ming dynasty, the final dramatic episode of a combination of circumstances that justified the loss of the celestial throne. First of all, a peasants' revolt threatened the empire of the interior, the rioters gaining access to the heart of the capital. Subsequently, the emperor hanged himself from a tree on the heights overlooking the Forbidden City, a tree that was then chained to expiate its sin! The love interest is provided by Chen Yuanyuan, beloved mistress of General Wu Sangui, defender of Shanhaiguan:

She sang and danced, as lovely as a flower . . .
Her charm eclipsed the brilliance of silk . . .
Her teeth were pearls and her eyes crystals . . .[69]

Then there were the Manchus, barbarians who had assimilated Chinese culture and had been attacking Chinese frontier posts with regularity for decades, waiting "beyond the passes" for the opportunity to cross them.

The protagonists, including the Great Wall, were all assembled; the drama could unfold.

Chen Yuanyuan was captured by the rebellious peasants who had gained control of Beijing. Her lover, guardian of the pass, called on the barbarians to help him release her. Once they had crossed the Great Wall and gained access to the Forbidden City, the Manchus ousted the Ming and founded the Qing dynasty.

The story of the Great Wall as built by the Ming ended in a classic tragedy for the dynasty. Instead of the adventures of an open world, the rulers of the capital stubbornly insisted on keeping the empire closed, through the progressive ossification of the frontier. All that remained was to see the emergence of myths and legends, to which the West largely contributed, out of the useless ruins.

The citadel of Jiayuguan, at the western end of the Gansu Corridor
Young Mongol camel drover

Mongolia of the steppes
Overleaf: Horses in the Mongolian steppe   193

The Great Wall at Jinshanling
202   Terra-cotta figurine of the Tang period

The Great Wall at Jinshanling
Guan Yu, guardian of the frontiers
Preceding pages: The Mongolian steppe at the foot of the Altai Mountains

Groom and Horses, painting of the Tang period
The Great Wall at Badaling

The Great Wall at Simatai

Sculpture of the Northern Wei period   219

There is something romantic about frontiers. They present the imagination with the reality and the dream. Travelers from Europe, more familiar with the expanse of the ocean than with prairies and steppes, those huge expanses of grassland, invoke freedom and comparisons with the sea: "The endless horizons on which huge flocks of clouds frolicked were rendered all the more comparable to a vast sea by the fact that they were dotted in places by tall watchtowers, irregularly positioned on the close-cropped steppes, surveying the plain like lighthouses."[89]

On the other hand, the continental borderlands of the Chinese world had no shore, and they crossed deserts, steppes, or huge masses of tumbled crags and peaks, the perfect setting for a drama. The Great Wall, placed in the midst of this scenery, becomes a concrete symbol of the cruelty and dictatorships that filled human hearts with terror.[90] Could we escape from this fascination charged with fear? We are impaled on a pendulum that moves back and forth; our perceptions betray us and suggest judgments that are as disconcerting as they are contradictory. "It is true that China has long been frightened by the barbarians, and it might have new reason to fear them in the future, but there have been times when the barbarians were just as frightened of China. We are in just such a phase at present. The barbarians are the ones who are in awe of China. That is why they have asked, and even insisted, on having the Great Wall rebuilt."[91] Seen from that angle, the wall could be said to be the combined effort of the Chinese and the barbarians, needing each of them in order to exist.

China is constantly reconstructing its past. Consequently, it has few authentic ancient monuments.[92] In this respect, the Great Wall is an exception, in that it runs the length of China and covers a history of more than two millennia. Erected to enhance the prestige of particular monarchs and dynasties, it has passed that prestige on to succeeding generations.

By making the Great Wall the symbol of modern China, the Chinese rulers simply associated the ambiguity of the one with the other, multiple and diverse, fragile but proud, never completed, constantly renewed, and always threatened.

I always felt myself enclosed on all sides by the Great Wall;
This wall of ancient bricks that is always being consolidated.
The old and the new conspire to confine all of us.
When will we cease to add new bricks to the Wall?
The Great Wall of China: a marvel and a malediction!

—LU XUN, 1935

Kirghiz caravan in the Afghan Pamir

Fresco of the Tang period in Shaanxi Province
224   The fortress of Zhenbeipu in Ningxia

Following pages: The Great Wall at Jinshanling   225

APPENDICES

Notes

1. We have used the official phonetic transcription (Pinyin), but retained the transcription used by the authors quoted.

2. Auguste Gilbert de Voisins, *Écrit en Chine* (Written in China), July 31, 1909 (Paris: You-Feng, 1987).

3. G. Margouliès, *Anthologie raisonnée de la littérature chinoise* (Annotated Anthology of Chinese Literature), (Paris: Payot, 1948). Lu Yu (1125–1210) was one of the most famous poets of the Southern Song dynasty (1127–1278).

4. Hexi ("West of the [Yellow] River") was used to designate different territories at different periods. During the Zhou dynasty (the Springs and Autumns and Fighting Kingdoms periods), it was at the southern end of the Yellow River, between what are now the provinces of Shanxi and Shaanxi. Under the Han and the Tang, it represented the territories now in the provinces of Gansu and Qinghai, west of the Yellow River. Under the northern dynasties, these were the territories situated west of the Lüliang Mountains (Lüliang Shan), including the east bank of the Yellow River in the province of Shanxi. In order to make matters more simple, later in the book Hexi will be used to designate what is now Gansu.

5. The word *Han* is used both for the dynasty and for the native Chinese, to distinguish them from the ethnic minorities of China.

6. In the twentieth century, Russian émigrés settled in large numbers in the northeast (Manchuria) and in Xinjiang. These settlements lasted for barely half a century.

7. The Yin Shan, "Dark Mountains," north of the meander in the Yellow River.

8. Paul Demiéville, ed., *Anthologie de la poésie chinoise classique* (Paris: Gallimard, 1962). Huliu Qin served under the Northern Qi dynasty (552–577). He was a famous horseman and archer who knew all the tricks of war against the Xiongnu.

9. Xi Hu, on Lake Hangzhou (now in Zhejiang Province), capital of the Song. On the period, see for example the book by J. Gernet, *La Vie quotidienne en Chine à la veille de l'invasion mongole, 1250–1276* (Paris: Hachette, 1959).

10. Demiéville, *Anthologie*. Poem by Uyang Xiu (1007–1072), a writer and poet and leading stateman under the Song, opponent of the reformer Wang Anshi.

11. Demiéville, *Anthologie*. Song of the Liang period (502–556), anonymous.

12. Marcel Granet, *La Civilisation chinoise* (Paris: Albin Michel, 1968); *Changcheng baike quanshu* (Encyclopedia of the Great Wall), Zhongguo Changcheng xuehui (Changchun: Jilin Province People's Publishing House, 1994).

13. In the late fourth century B.C.E. the armies of the Qin state conquered the barbarian lands that lay to the west of their territory, beyond the Liupan Shan range that separated the upper valley of the river Wei from the Yellow River. This gave them access to Lanzhou, where a command post had been established in 280 B.C.E. at Longxi (now known as Lintao), on the Tao He River. They probably found a Chinese colony already there, since it was both a port for river traffic at the upper reach of the Yellow River and the point of arrival for caravans from central Asia. The Qin people suddenly found themselves in contact with the distant West. The influence and fame of Qin expanded from this point, and it is very possible that this is why the name was adopted in the West to designate the civilized inhabitants of the Far East, the Cina or Mahacina of the epic poets of India, the peoples of the place called Sina by the Greeks.

14. Sima Qian (145–86 B.C.E.) lived under the Western Han.

15. Barbarian tribes of the north and west, neighbors of the Qin kingdom.

16. Lintao: now Min Xian, in Gansu, south of Lanzhou.

17. Liaodong, "East of the Liao" (the river), in Liaoning Province.

18. Chapter 88 of Sima Quian, *Historical Records*, trans. Raymond Dawson (Oxford; New York: Oxford University Press, 1994). Chapter 110 repeats some of the explanations by providing others. Thus Meng Tian, "having defeated the Xiongnu, established forty-four fortified cities overlooking the riverbanks and completed the defense fortifications by using the mountains as natural barriers, cutting through valleys, and building ramparts and other structures wherever necessary."

19. Successive discoveries since 1974 have begun to give an idea of the monumental dimensions of the tomb, near present-day Xi'an. Descriptions in Sima Qian, *Historical Records*, suggest that future excavations will lead to discoveries just as spectacular.

20. Victor Segalen, "Peintures," in *Œuvres complètes* (Paris: Robert Laffont, 1995).

21. Sima Qian, *Historical Records*.

22. The Wei is a tributary of the middle Yellow River, flowing from west to east, in the middle of what is now the province of Shaanxi. Several dynasties, including the Qin, Western Han, and Tang, established a capital city on the south bank, near present-day Xi'an.

23. Karl Jettmar, *L'Art des steppes* (Paris: Albin Michel, 1964); René Grousset, *L'Empire des steppes* (Paris: Payot, 1965), appendix on animal portraits.

24. Marcel Granet, *La Pensée chinoise* (Paris: Albin Michel, 1950).

25. Li Po (701–762), "They are fighting at the southern end of the Wall." Margouliès, *Anthologie*.

26. The policy of *heqin*, defined and practiced by the Han. Other dynasties applied similar policies of good relations based on trade and on subjugation, as did the Tang with their *jimi* (policy of control).

27. Prosopopea inspired by and developed from a short extract concerning Tumen and Modun in Sima Qian, *Historical Records*, and from poems of the Han period.

28. Ferghana: region located between the Tian Shan and Pamir ranges.

29. Bactria: now northern Afghanistan.

30. Ili: river that flows west of the Tian Shan range, flowing into Lake Balkash.

31. Tian Shan: "Celestial Mountains," from the Pamir Mountains to the Gobi Desert.

32. This phenomenon is due to the presence of *Parafilaria multipapillosa*, a parasite common in these regions. It lives just under the skin and produces droplets of blood that mingle with sweat when the horse is exercised in summer. See Bertrand Langlois, "L'Élevage du cheval en Union soviétique," *Bulletin technique du département de génétique animale*, no. 40 (1986), Institut national de la recherche agronomique.

33. Yongdeng: northwest of Lanzhou.

MANY MAPS OF CHINA show the line of the Great Wall, but they are rarely accurate. Most of them merely indicate the sections of the wall built by the Ming. Even in specialist books, the indications are vague, and may even be contradictory. The *Encyclopedia of the Great Wall* (*Changcheng baike quanshu* in Chinese; 1,220 pages) does not contain a single map of the wall under any dynasty. The map overleaf is inspired by several works in Chinese, some of which contain maps of walls and the Great Wall erected in various dynasties. The juxtaposition of these maps shows that over the centuries, from Mongolia to the outskirts of the capital, the defense of the walls was an almost constant preoccupation. The maze of earthworks and brick and stone structures suggests that the name "walls of the north" would be more appropriate than "Great Wall," since the latter has been so misused as to imply a single and continuous structure.

The present tracing of the wall is based on the following records:

- Gao Wang, *Bolan changcheng fengcai* (Beijing, 1991).
- Gao Wang, *Neimanggu changcheng shihua* (Huhehuote, 1991).
- Guo Moruo, ed., *Zhongguo shigao dituji*, 2 vols. (Shanghai, 1996).
- *Hebei sheng pudong dituji* (Beijing, 1994).
- Tan Qixiang, ed., *Zhongguo lishi dituji*, 8 vols. (Shanghai, 1982).

The map does not show:

- subordinate structures alongside the wall, especially near the passes and big cities, since the scale does not allow for greater accuracy;
- walls built in the south of the provinces of Hebei, Henan, and Shandong during the Fighting Kingdoms period between the rival states of Qi, Zhao, Wei, Han, and Chu.

REPUBLIC OF MONGOLIA

GOBI DESERT

EASTERN ALTAI

XINJIANG

QILIAN SHAN

QINGHAI

AUTONOMOUS

CHIN

LANG SHAN

YIN S

PLATEAU

OF THE ORDOS

HELAN SHAN

NINGXIA

SHAANXI

Kyakhta
Darhan
Boulgan
ULAN-BATOR
Arvayheer
Sayns
Dalanzadgad
Eijin Qi
Hami
Yumenguan
(First Jade Gate)
Dunhuang
Yumen
Jiayuguan
Jiuquan
Jiayuguan
Gaotai
Zhangye
Shandan
Hela Hu
Wuwei ★
Koukou Nor
Xining
Huang Shui
Guyuan
Wuyuan
Linhe
Baoti
Wuda
Dongsh
Shizuishan
Zhenbeipu
Ningxia ★
(Yinchuan)
Lingwu
Yanch
Wuding
Hengsh
Yulir
Anbian
Yan'an
Fu Xiar

95°   50°   100°   105°

45°

40°

Dynasties

(simplified list)

Chronology of the Construction of the Great Wall

722–475 B.C.E.
Springs and Autumns (Zuochuan) period.

685–645 B.C.E. | Construction of defensive walls by the Kingdom of Qi (now Shandong Province) along the southern frontier of the Kingdom of Chu.

656 B.C.E. | Construction of fortifications (*fangcheng*) by the Kingdom of Chu (now Henan Province) along the western, northern, and eastern frontiers for protection against Qi. The Han River to the south constituted a "great wall of water" (*shui changcheng*).

475–221 B.C.E.
Fighting Kingdoms (Zhanguo) period

461–409 B.C.E. | Construction of walls by the Kingdom of Qin (now southern Shaanxi) for protection against the advance of the Jin state west of the Yellow River.

369 B.C.E. | On the northern frontier with Jin and Zhao, the Zhongshan state erects walls in the Taihang Shan range, west of what is now Hebei, from Longquanguan in the north, stretching around 300 miles (480 km) in a southerly direction. The wall would nevertheless be conquered by Zhao in 296.

361–358 B.C.E. | To protect itself against Qin in the east and from the barbarians (the western Rong) in the north, Wei builds a wall stretching for about 650 miles (1050 km), from what is now Huaxian (Shaanxi) in the north, on the western shore of the Yellow River.

355 B.C.E. | Wei builds another wall in what is now Henan, about 400 miles long, as protection against attacks from Qin.

334 B.C.E. | Yan, in what is now northern Hebei, builds a wall in the south of its territory to protect it from Qi, Zhao, and Qin. This is called the "Yishui Wall," named for the river whose course it follows.

333 B.C.E. | Zhao, covering what are now the provinces of Hebei and Henan, builds a wall to protect itself from Wei.

300 B.C.E. | Prince Wuling of Zhao, who borrows some of the techniques of the mounted archers of his turbulent neighbors, the Hu barbarians (clothing, riding tackle, bows), also builds a wall along the northern frontier of his territory, from which is now called Xuanhua (northwest of Beijing, in Hebei) right up to Mongolia, in the Lang Shan range. It stretches for more than 1,300 *lis*.

272 B.C.E. | King Zhaoxiang of Qin builds several walls of about 4,000 *lis*, from what is now Gansu in the southeast, passing close to Yulin, to the northeastern corner of the meander of the Yellow River, in order to contain the incursions of the eastern Hu barbarians.

254 B.C.E. | To protect itself from the incursions of the eastern Hu nomads, Yan builds walls along the northern frontier, in what is now Zhangjiakou, right up to the province of Liaoning, a distance of about 2,400 *lis.*

214 B.C.E. | Qin Shi Huangdi, the first unifying emperor of China, sends his general Meng Tian to build a wall along the northern frontier to protect the territory from incursions by the Xiongnu nomads. Several sections of wall erected by previous rulers are used to form a long defense line along the western and northern frontiers of the empire. In the west, in what is now Gansu, the wall runs from Min Xian (Lintao) to Lanzhou, from the southwest to the northeast of the meander of the Yellow River, on the right-hand shore of the Yellow River. The defenses are completed by a line of fortifications. North of the river, starting from the Lang Shan range, in what is now Inner Mongolia, the wall turns east, passing near Wuchang and Jining, north of what is now Zhangjiakou, and from Chifeng it continues into Liaoning, redescending to the Yalu River north of Shenyang and ending at what is now Pyongyang. The defenses extend over about "ten thousand *lis.*" This line of fortifications is completed in around 210 B.C.E.

221–206 B.C.E.
The Qin dynasty,
first unification of China

204 B.C.E. | Two years after establishing the new Han dynasty, the emperor Taizong causes the Zhaoxiang Wall to be built from Qin, to contain the Xiongnu on the northwestern frontier.

130 B.C.E. | Emperor Wudi of the Western Han launches an offensive against the Xiongnu and has the wall rebuilt, from Zhangjiakou in what is now Hebei up to Huhehuote in Inner Mongolia.

127 B.C.E. | Emperor Wudi sends Huo Qubing to conquer the territories west of the Yellow River (Hexi). He establishes the command posts of Wuwei and Jiuquan and begins building a wall in the Gansu Corridor, thus extending westward the wall built by Qin Shi Huangdi.

111 B.C.E. | Emperor Wudi establishes new command posts at Zhangye and Dunhuang and continues the building of the wall from Jiuquan to Yumenguan.

102 B.C.E. | Emperor Wudi accompanies his policy of contact with the territories in the west with an extension of the wall beyond Yumenguan, right up to Lobnor. He establishes advance garrisons in what is now Xinjiang, along the routes that become known as the Silk Road. In the same year he reinforces the northern frontier's defenses by adding two more walls behind the first one (*Changcheng fuxian* or *Wudi waicheng,* "the outer wall of Wudi") north of the Yin Shan range. The walls stretch as far as the Altai Mountains in the west. The two walls lie at a distance of between six and sixty miles from each other. The southern wall descends and penetrates westward in what is now Gansu.

206 B.C.E.–186 C.E.
Western and Eastern Han dynasties

239

36–45 C.E. | To resist a new thrust by the Xiongnu, in 36 C.E., Eastern Han emperor Guang Wudi sends troops to the northern frontier to strengthen part of the fortifications. Then in what is now Shanxi, between Yanggao and Datong, he builds four sections of fortifications in northern Shaanxi, from Shanxi in 37 C.E. and from Hebei in 38 C.E. In 45 C.E., he adds further reinforcements.

186–580
The three kingdoms (Wei in the north, Shu in Sichuan, Wu in the south) enjoy a brief reunification between the Western Jin (265–313) and the northern dynasties, the most important of which are the Northern Wei (380–550) and the Southern Wei.

423 | The Northern Wei dynasty is forced to resist the Rouran nomads in the north and the Qidan in the northeast. A wall is built from Chifeng in the east to Wuyuan in the west, in what is now Inner Mongolia, a distance of around 2,000 *lis*.

446 | Northern Wei emperor Tai Wudi sends 100,000 men out to build a wall called the Jishang Saiwei, "Rampart of the Imperial Lands," to contain the Rouran thrust into the region of what is now Datong. This structure extends southwest from Juyongguan, near Beijing, to Lingqiu, southeast of Datong, and westward from Pingxingguan (Shanxi, west of Lingqiu) to Hequ, on the east bank of the Yellow River, a distance of about 1,000 *lis*.

484 | The annals of the Northern Wei mention the construction of a wall north of the six cities (*zhen*), though no trace of it has been found.

543 | The Eastern Wei build a wall to contain the Rouran. Constructed in only forty days, it runs for 150 *lis*, from Jingle, northeast of Taiyuan (now Shanxi), northeastward to Daixian.

552–577 | After annexing the Eastern Wei territories, the Northern Qi dynasty governs what are now the provinces of Hebei, Henan, Shanxi, and Shandong. In the north, it has to contend with the incursions of the Tujue, Rouran, and Qidan nomads. A wall is built in 552, from Fenyang, on the west bank of the Fen, to Wuzhai, northwest of Shanxi. In the same year, the wall is rebuilt from Juyongguan to Datong. In 556 more parts of the wall are built, from Datong eastward to the sea, over a total area of 3,000 *lis*. In 557 another (interior) wall is built from Shuoxian, in northern Shanxi, to the outskirts of Pingxingguan, a distance of 400 *lis*.

To contain the expansion of the Northern Zhou eastward, in 563 the Northern Qi build a 200-*li* wall beside the Taihang Shan, from Jiyuan north of Luoyang, in what is now Henan, to Fuping, in what is now Hebei. Between 564 and 577, the existing sectors of the wall are reinforced several times.

579 | The Northern Zhou defeat the Western Wei and expand their territory until they rule a land that covers the present-day provinces of Hebei, Shanxi, and Shandong. To contain the threat from the Tujue and Qidan nomads on their northern border, they build a wall between Yanmenguan (Shanxi) and Jieshi (Hebei).

581–608 | After reunifying China, Emperor Wen of the Sui dynasty has to confront the incursions of the Tujue. At first he merely mends the wall in Shanxi, but in 585 he builds a new wall from Lingwu (now Ningxia) on the Yellow River to Hengshan (northern Shaanxi), a distance of around 700 *lis*. In 586 he sends 110,000 men to rebuild the wall on the northern frontier of what are now the provinces of Gansu, Ningxia, and Shaanxi. Emperor Yang of the Sui reinforces some parts of the wall in 607, between Yulin (Shaanxi) and northeastern Datong (Shanxi), and in 608, between Yulin and Wuyuan (Inner Mongolia). The Sui dynasty maintains several sections of the wall that had been built previously, but does not build new ones.

1058 | To protect itself from the Nuzhen, the Liao dynasty builds walls in the northeast, in the region of the Songhua (Soungari) and Heilong Rivers.

1148–1199 | After eliminating the Liao and Song dynasties, the Nuzhen create the Jin dynasty in 1115. They erect walls on their northern frontier, first in 1148 near what is now Baicheng, in western Jilin. More work is done in 1163 and 1181 on the northwest frontier. In 1190, during the reign of Mingchang, the Jin build two systems of walls to defend themselves against the Mongol incursions, on their northwestern and northern border. In the north, the walls extend through what is now the province of Heilongjiang, northwest of greater Hing'an (Khingan). This is the wall known as the Wushu Changcheng, "Great Wall of Wushu," the Jinyuan Bianbao, "frontier fortification of Jinyuan" or the Mingchang Jiucheng, "Old Mingchang Wall." It covers a thousand *lis*. To the south, the other wall covers three thousand *lis*, from the meander of the Yellow River in Inner Mongolia to the Soungari River. This is the Jinnei Changcheng, "Inner Wall of the Jin," or Mingchang Xincheng, "New Wall of Mingchang."

1368–1644 | When the Ming dynasty is established in 1368, no wall exists to mark the frontier. For more than two hundred years the Ming constantly build and rebuild a system of defenses on their northern frontiers that becomes increasingly complex, as a defense against incursions by the Mongols and the Nuzhen (Manchus).

From the early years of his reign, Emperor Hongwu establishes an initial line of garrisons (the "eight external garrisons") and a second line of fortresses and signal towers, with a more defensive role, north of Beijing and Shanxi, especially in the most important mountain passes. This second line takes almost the identical course to the future Ming wall. In 1376 the army is sent to reinforce the main passes, those of Gubeikou, Juyongguan, Xifengkou, and Songjingguan, but no new wall is built.

The outpost garrisons of the steppe are abandoned in the reigns of Yongle (1403–25) and Xuande (1426–36). Historians have never found satisfactory explanations for this decision, which will have serious strategic consequences.

581–618
Sui dynasty

618–917
Tang dynasty. The empire controls the nomadic populations well beyond the walls built by previous dynasties.

907–960
The Five Dynasties, including the Liao (founded in 937). The Qidan barbarians from the northeast settle in northern China.

960–1276
The Song dynasty first settles in the center, then in the south, but is not interested in the Great Wall.

1276–1368
The Yuan dynasty.
This Mongolian empire covered a vast area from Asia to Europe, well beyond the Great Wall. The Yuan merely maintained a few border fortresses to control entry.

1368–1644
Ming dynasty

The battle of Tumu against the Mongols in 1449 is a grave defeat for the Ming, who decide to reinforce their defenses in more than fifty passes, including Zixingguan and Juyongguan. The Mongols take over the abandoned Ordos loop and live a nomadic existence there.

The Ming build their first set of walls (of double thickness) in the southern Ordos between 1474 and the mid-sixteenth century, from the Yellow River to the heights of what is now Ningxia, right up to northeastern Shaanxi on the opposite bank of the Yellow River. From the late fifteenth century onward, many isolated fortifications are built over an area stretching from Jiayuguan in the far west to Juyongguan, north of Beijing. It is only from the sixteenth century that a continuous system of defenses is gradually built up from west to east, as the Mongol attacks move in an encircling movement. This system is not termed "Great Wall," but *Jiu Bianzhen*, the "nine frontier garrisons." As a result of the northern frontier raids by the Altan Khan and his incursion into China right up to the walls of Beijing, thus demonstrating the vulnerability of the system of defenses, the most frenzied period of the wall-building activity begins, lasting from the late sixteenth through the early seventeenth century.

Juyongguan (Juyong Pass), northwest of Beijing, has been fortified since the Han dynasty, but the Ming actually build a wall across it. After the Battle of Tumu, several walls are added. The Badaling Wall dates from 1539 through 1582. From 1569 through 1583, General Qi Jiguang, commander of the Jizhou garrison (one of the "nine frontier garrisons"), orders the building of the Juyongguan Wall to the sea. This wall, with its regularly spaced towers linked by a continuous wall, becomes the model for constructing other sectors of the Great Wall, especially in the Xuanfu (Xuanhua) region.

A first fort was built on the Shanhaiguan coastal plain under the Northern Qi. Another fortification is built by the Ming in 1382. New work is undertaken, especially after 1551. The walls date from the late sixteenth century. In 1571, thanks to the fact that the pass has regained its strategic importance, Shanhaiguan becomes a separate command from that of Jizhou.

At Jiayuguan, at the opposite, western end of the Great Wall, the first fort is built in 1372. Gradually other features, such as towers and gates, are added between 1495 and 1507. The mounting insecurity of this section of the frontier leads to a reinforcement of the structure, starting in 1539, and eventually takes on the dimensions and form that it retains to the present day.

On the eve of the Manchu invasion of northern China, in 1644, work continues to reinforce or complete the Great Wall.

1644–1911
Qing (Manchu) dynasty

The Qing empire extends beyond the Ming Wall. In order to deter non-Manchu tribes from migrating to Manchuria, the Qing build the "Barrier of the Poplars" (also known as the "Barrier of the Willows" or "Barrier of the Stakes"), in what are now the provinces of Liaoning and Jilin. It indicates the frontier that must not be crossed, but consists merely of a low mud levee planted with poplar or willow trees and backed with a ditch. The willows are later replaced by elms or by a mere row of stakes. The Barrier of the Poplars consists of two sections. The first, based on the Great Wall at Shanhaiguan, stretches northeastward to Kaiyuan (the northern part of what is now Liaoning), then turns southward to the mouth of the Yalu River. It has sixteen gates, named after the locations closest to them. It is 1,950 *lis* (about 700 miles) long. The second wall is reinforced by the first, northwest of Kaiyuan, and stretches northeastward, east of Changchun, ending beyond Songhua Jiang (Soungari), in northern Jilin. It has four gates and is 690 *lis* (about 200 miles) long.

The Manchus of the Qing dynasty appear to have used for part of the route of their wall the old barrier erected by the Ming. The line is not identical, however, because the Ming barrier turns southward at around what is now Fuxin, just north of Niuzhuang (on the left bank of the Hun He River), then turns north above Kaiyuan and descends again to the sea, passing east of Fushun. The western route of the "Barrier of the Poplars," from Shanhaiguan to its most northern reach, fixed the easternmost limit of Mongol territory, beyond which the barbarians were forbidden to venture.

PAGES 30–31 | The Yellow River at Jia Xian, in Shaanxi Province.

Most historians agree that the cradle of Chinese civilization is the central Yellow River region, in what are now the provinces of Shanxi and Shaanxi, and more specifically in the Fen and Wei Valleys. Civilization spread outward to other regions, where it encountered "barbarians" who were progressively assimilated into Chinese culture. Their gradual mastery of cultivation techniques turned them into sedentary farmers who were strangers to the nearby world of the steppe.

Neolithic people appear to have discovered how to smelt and use metal in the central Yellow River region, which includes the Ordos. This gave them a clear advantage over other groups: "They thus opened up an immense historical perspective: the creation of the concepts of 'Chinese' and 'barbarians'" (Owen Lattimore).

PAGE 32 | The Yellow River upstream of Lanzhou (Gansu).

PAGE 33 | Noria on the Yellow River in the region of Lanzhou, Gansu.

PAGE 34 | Turkish or Mongolian prisoner. Fifteenth-century miniature, Topkapı Museum, Istanbul.

PAGE 35 | The Great Wall at Jinshanling.

PAGE 36 | Han farmer.

The Han are the native Chinese, as opposed to the inhabitants of China whose ethnicity (nationality, or *minzu*) is diverse, and includes Mongols, Tibetans, and Turks (Uighur, Kazakh, and so on). The Han Chinese account for about 92 percent of the total population. The original inhabitants were called *huaxia*, "an islet of civilization in the midst of barbarians." They occupied the most fertile valleys of the central Yellow River, including the Wei Valley. As descendants of the population living under the Xia, Shang, and Zhou dynasties (of which only the last was in historic times), they are said to have been responsible for the oldest signs of Chinese civilization, which are three or four thousand years old: writing, bronze objects, religious rituals, and so on. According to Chinese historians, the *huaxia* were identifiable from the eighth century B.C.E. Gradually, especially during the period of the Fighting Kingdoms (between the fifth and third centuries B.C.E.), neighboring barbarian tribes assimilated into the civilized population, thus swelling their ranks. The unification of the empire in 221 B.C.E. by Qin Shi Huangdi and the accompanying measures reinforced the homogeneity of a large sector of the population of China. Over the following four centuries, the Han dynasties continued the work of unification that had been begun under Qin Shi Huangdi.

Under the Western Han, the barbarian populations of the frontiers continued to call their neighbors who manned the garrisons Qinren, "Qin's men" (of the Qin state). They only gradually became known as Hanren, "Han's men" (of the Han empire), or simply the Han. After the fall of the Eastern Han, the name stuck, even though it went through changes over the centuries. Until relatively recently (the Yuan dynasty), the distinction between the Han and the others, or the assimilation of other inhabitants into the Han, was based on the two different cultures, agrarian and sedentary versus pastoral and nomadic, the foundations of which date back to the Qin and Han dynasties.

PAGE 37 | Detail of a battle scene. Painting of the Ming period, Topkapi Museum, Istanbul.

PAGE 40 | Groom. Detail of a terra cotta statuette of the Tang dynasty. Museum of the History of the Revolution, Beijing.

PAGE 41 | Brick wall at Jiaoshan, in Hebei Province.

Near the "(Dragon's) Horn Mountain," about a mile north of Shanhaiguan.

PAGE 42–43 | The Jiaolou Tower (Horn Tower), on the Jiaoshan Wall.

This tower stands on the easternmost peaks of the Yan Shan, dominating the coastal plain above Shanhaiguan. Liaoning is on the left, and beyond it, the great Manchurian plain; to the right is the northern Chinese plain.

This is an interesting example of the various inter-actions between the peoples of the northern frontier, both Chinese and barbarians. Huang Zongdao was a painter who lived during the Northern Song dynasty (960–1127). He specialized in scenes from the daily lives of non-Han peoples, taking his inspiration from the tenth-century painters Li Zanhua and Hu Gui, who were themselves mem-bers of the Qidan (Khitan) tribes, famous for their eques-trian paintings. In this hunting scene, Huang Zongdao has painted a young huntsman riding a sturdy, highspirited mount with a thick coat, the typical "Mongolian horse." He has just shot an arrow at a stag. It is hard to be sure whether the rider is a Qidan, as his harness would lead one to believe, or whether he is a Han, as his long nails and buckskin hat would indicate.

The province of Shanxi (the Mountainous West) lies east and north of the Yellow River. It is a mountainous region, whose Taihang Shan range separates it from the great northern plain. In the west, the Lüliang Shan range runs parallel to the river, and the loess landscape is covered in deep ravines caused by waterways, including the Fen River. The official phonetic (*pinyin*) transcriptions of the neighboring provinces of Shanxi and Shaanxi are almost identical except that the latter has two *a*'s. Shaanxi lies to the west of Shanxi in the meander of the Yellow River.

Shaanxi (called Shenxi in transcriptions other than *pinyin*) was originally known as the Qin region (just like the first imperial dynasty) in the Springs and Autumns period, and that of the Fighting Kingdoms, then as Neishe during the first imperial dynasty, Guannei (Within the Passes) under the Tang, and Shaanxilu (the Western Road to Shaan, the name for what is now Sanmenxia in south-ern Shanxi) under the Song. The present name was first adopted under the Qing dynasty.

Loess covers a vast area, including almost the whole of Shaanxi, southern Shanxi, part of western Henan, east-ern Gansu, and southern Ningxia. This is also the geo-graphical area that covers the basin of the middle Yellow River, where Chinese civilization first developed in the Wei, Fen, and Luo Rivers. The soil is not particularly fertile, but it is easy to work, as it has no dense forest cover that needs to be cleared first. People originally lived in holes dug into the loess soil, but these dwellings were replaced by caves that were easily dug in the cliffs and were cool in summer and comfortable in winter. No doubt these shelters also helped the inhabitants to protect themselves from marauders.

Loess is an extremely porous soil that absorbs water quickly. The moisture retained then nourishes plant growth. The natural covering of a loess region is grass, with brush and shrubs in the valleys. The slow accumulation of depos-its increases the thickness of the topsoil, enabling grass to grow in successive layers. The plants that have been buried no longer grow, but they increase the porosity of the soil and enrich it. Loess fields are constantly being fertilized even in the absence of manure, as long as there is enough water, so irrigation is essential for cultivation in such re-gions. It is thus easy to understand the importance of the type of society that prevailed, in particular the need for cooperation between farmers to ensure that the soil was well watered.

Any expansion of the growing area depended on the presence of water and using it in the service of agriculture. From the cradle of civilization, progress naturally spread to the other regions with a loess soil, then into the north-ern plain and southward to the Yangzi (Chang) basin, when greater resources became available.

North of the loess plateau and what became the line of the Great Wall, the landscape suddenly changes. The system of agriculture adopted for the loess valleys could not be extended here, with the exception of a few irrigable sections near the Yellow River, and then only at certain times of the year.

PAGES 68–69 | Flocks being driven home near Zhenbeipu, in the Autonomous Region of Ningxia. (*See also p. 224.*)

PAGES 70–71 | Bronze horses and chariots, Eastern Han period. Private collection.

PAGE 72 | Kazakh hunter with his tame eagle, Bayan-Ölgi, Mongolia.

The distant ancestors of the Kazakhs were the various nomadic tribes, called Wusun, Xiongnu, Yueche, etc., who roamed through central Asia as far as northern China. According to written sources, they were displaced between the third and eighth centuries by Turkish-Mongolian peoples, such as the Tuoba, Turks, and Uighurs. The Kazakhs originated from various Turkish tribes that split up when the Timuride dynasty collapsed, identifying themselves with that name from the sixteenth century. They are believed to have cultural links with the peoples who lived in northwestern China and the Altai since the second millennium B.C.E. Their socioeconomic structure is based on nomadic husbandry.

The Kazakhs were either allies or vassals, with varying degrees of loyalty, of the Russian empire until the mid-eighteenth century. A complex relationship developed between the Kazakhs, who owed allegiance to the tsar, and the Qing empire, which wanted to eliminate the western Mongols, who were also enemies of the Kazakhs. Like their predecessors, the Qing were interested in acquiring horses for military purposes, and because the Kazakhs were important horse dealers, they were invited to hold horse fairs on the ill-defined frontiers of the Chinese empire, especially in the valley of the Ili.

A variety of factors, most important of which was the Russian thrust into central Asia, encouraged the Kazakhs to settle closer to the Chinese border when the frontier began to be fixed on the basis of treaties entered into by the Russian and Chinese empires after 1864. Certain Kazakh families thus settled in the Ili Valley, in the northern half of Xinjiang, and in the Altai region, including the northern part of this mountain range, which lies inside Outer Mongolia, then a Chinese possession.

In 1990 there were about 10 million Kazakhs, most of whom were living in Kazakhstan (6.5 million), China (1.1 million, mainly in Xinjiang), the former Soviet republics in central Asia, and Mongolia (113,000). In China, the Kazakhs live mainly in the the Ili Valley, in the province of Gansu, and west of Qinghai. They have inhabited these last two provinces since the mid-1930s.

PAGE 73 | The Great Wall at Mutianyu, north of Beijing.

PAGES 76–77 | Kirghiz caravan trader. Afghan Pamir.

The Kirghiz, like the Kazakhs, are descended from Turkish-Mongolian tribes that emerged as nations during the decline of the Timuride empire. The Kirghiz are scattered over southern Siberia in the Pamir range. They are mainly mountain dwellers and shepherds tending flocks of sheep, camels, and yaks. The Tian Shan range forms a natural barrier between the two groups of Kirghiz, those of the eastern slope, the Chinese side, and those of the western side, which is either Afghan or in what was once Soviet territory and is now divided into Tadjikistan, Kyrgyzstan, and Kazakhstan.

Since the nineteenth century, whenever the political climate made communication possible and desirable, the Kirghiz moved back and forth across the territories, always trying to preserve their way of life and their freedom.

PAGE 80 | Portrait of an officer, detail of an enameled terra-cotta of the Tang period, a *yong* figurine. Height: 28½ in. (73 cm). Museum of the History of the Revolution, Beijing.

PAGE 81 | Horse's head, detail of a terra cotta of the Tang, polychrome glaze. Height: 26½ in. (68 cm). Museum of the History of the Revolution, Beijing.

PAGES 82–83 | The Ming Wall at Mutianyu, north of Beijing.

Stone and brick. The stone gargoyles face the interior of the pass.

PAGE 84 | Buddhist monk.

PAGE 85 | **The Sangim River and the Buddhist caves of Bezeklik, near Turfan, Xinjiang. Photograph by Romain Michaud.**

The route leading west from the Gansu Corridor was protected under the Ming dynasty by the Great Wall as far as Yumenguan or Jiayuguan; it ends at Xinjiang. This was the route taken by Buddhist pilgrims visiting India, starting about two thousand years ago. From Datong or Luoyang to the Tarim basin via Dunhuang, caves and monasteries line the road that skirts the Tibetan mountain range to the west. In 629, under the Tang, Xuan Zang, one of the most famous Buddhist pilgrims, disobeyed an imperial order that prohibited travel outside the empire and took the road westward to India. At first he followed the line of the Great Wall (erected by the Han), having been given information about it before his departure: "It is after the widest part that the Jade Gate was created, through which one is forced to pass and which marks the western frontier. To the northwest, outside this gate, there are five signaling towers manned by watchmen who serve as lookouts. They are at intervals of a hundred *lis*. There is neither water nor greenery in the gaps between them. Beyond the five towers lie the Mojiayan [Gobi] desert and the frontiers of the kingdom of Yiwu [the kingdom of Hami]." As he reached the first signal tower, Xuan Zang was almost hit by an arrow, but finally received assistance and advice from the commander of the outpost to help him on his way. After crossing the Gobi Desert and reaching Yiwu (Hami), he continued on to Gaochang (Turfan), where he was received by the monarch and lodged in a convent near the palace. Etiemble, ed., *L'Inde du Bouddha, vue par des pèlerins chinois sous la dynasty Tang* (Paris: Calmann-Lévy, 1968).

PAGE 86 | **Buddhist monk on a pilgrimage. Tenth-century painting on silk, Dunhuang Caves, Gansu. Musée Guimet, Paris.**

PAGE 88 | **Bactrian camel. Terra-cotta funerary object (*mingqi*) of the Sui period. Height: 19 in. (49 cm). Private collection.**

PAGES 88–89 | **Kirghiz caravan on the roof of the world. Afghan Pamir.**

The Afghan Pamir has long offered a route between Iran and Afghanistan in the west and the Chinese world in the east, especially through the Wakkan Corridor. Caravans took the southern Silk Road from the Chinese capital, passed along the Gansu Corridor and the fortifications or towers of the Great Wall, and reached the Stone Tower (Tash Kurgan) before crossing the "high Pamirs." Merchants, pilgrims, and other travelers have passed this way for centuries.

According to certain historians, rare and luxurious goods not produced in China but greatly desired by the court had to be procured from distant regions. This does not explain, however, so great a desire to embark on long journeys and obtain goods that were difficult to preserve. The main motivation, at a time when the imperial power had the means to fulfill its ambitions, was the opportunity of establishing relations for strategic purposes with the peoples living beyond the lands of the hostile nomads. It was a sort of extension by other means, whether offensive or defensive, of the Great Wall.

PAGES 90–91 | **Kirghiz camel drover crossing a mountain pass. Afghan Pamir.**

The camels used by the drovers on the Silk Road, an image that has become a cliché, were Bactrian camels. They are powerful and hardy, and for centuries were the ideal mount or pack animal for crossing the vast arid or semi-arid expanses from the Pamir range to Mongolia. At high altitude, when using the mountain passes in the Pamir or Tian Shan ranges, the Kirghiz preferred to use yaks or horses.

In 1906 Sir Aurel Stein took the ancient road from the Afghan slopes via the sources of the Oxus (Amu Daria) to the Chinese mountains, noting that this route had always been used by traders in summer.

The quantity of goods carried was small, however, because trading along this route was far less frequent than along the routes to the north of the Tian Shan and even through the Himalayas to India (and what is now Pakistan).

PAGES 92–93 | Bactria camels. Terra-cotta figures from the Tang dynasty. Private collections.

PAGE 94 | Brick wall in the Huanghuacheng (Yellow Flower) region, north of Beijing.

PAGE 95 | Winter landscape (detail). Fifteenth-century Turkish-Mongolian miniature, extract from the *Album of the Conqueror*. Topkapi Museum, Istanbul.

PAGES 98–99 | Loess landscape in Shaanxi, between Luochuan and Fuxian.

PAGES 102–3 | The Ming Wall at Jinshanling, near the Gubeikou Pass.

The Gubeikou Pass was originally called Hubeikou, "Northern Tiger Pass," being named for a small nearby peak called Wohu Shan, "Mountain of the Sitting Tiger."

The first fortifications of the pass, which cross the narrow valley of the river Chao, date from the Northern Qi dynasty (550–577). Nothing remains of these earth and stone constructions. The pass is an important crossing point, first mentioned in 986 under the Liao (Qidan or Khitan Tartars). In 1214, under the Jin (Nuzhen Tartars, 1115–1234), it was known as Tiemenguan ("Pass of the Iron Gates"). Under the Ming, Gubeikou, like Juyongguan, became strategically important in the defense of Beijing, the capital. Fortifications capable of containing a garrison of several thousand men were built there from 1378, and a wall was built to the west for about 600 yards, and east for about a mile (the Jinshanling section).

In 1550 Altan, the Mongol khan who mainly exerted pressure on the Ming fortification lines in the Ordos and the Datong region, moved his troops northeast to an area that was less well defended. His Mongol cavalry followed the valley of the river Chao to Gubeikou, passing through the Chinese lines through minor roads and valleys. Two days later, the Mongols sacked the city of Dongzhou (now Dongxian), in the plain east of Beijing. A few hundred of them then advanced to the very foot of the Walled City, at the Andingmen Gate. This incident is known in Chinese history as Gengshu Zhi Yi, "the Battle to Keep the Frontier." It proved decisive for the imperial court, persuading it to extend the wall eastward.

Under the Qing dynasty, while the Manchus dominated the Mongols, Gubeikou remained one of the few routes by which the Mongolian plateau and the northeast could be accessed, especially to reach Chengde, the summer capital built by the emperor Kangxi.

PAGES 104, 105, and 107 | Earthen wall at Bataicun, in Shanxi, on the road to Ninglukou, northwest of Datong.

PAGE 106 | Woman playing a *wude*. Terra-cotta of the Northern Qi dynasty (550–577). Museum of the History of the Revolution, Beijing.

Yong statuette, a funerary object *(mingqi)*. The *piba* is a Chinese musical instrument known to have existed at least since the Qin dynasty, but other musical instruments, such as this *wude*, or *piba chuxiang*, were introduced into China from central Asia during the period of the Five Dynasties. From the early fifth century, China began to import music from central Asia on a large scale. This is particularly true of the Tang dynasty, a period during which the music of the city-states of Kashgar, Kucha, Khotan, Bukhara, and Turfan constituted half of the official "Ten Types of Music" (laid down in 640–42) at the court of Chang'an. See *Concise Oxford Dictionary of Music* (New York: Oxford University Press, 1996).

PAGE 108 | Ladies of the court. Terra-cotta figurines of the Tang dynasty. Private collection.

Yong representing rather plump ladies of the court, like the figure of the concubine Yang Guifei, favorite of the emperor Xuanzong. (See caption for p. 5.)

PAGE 109 | Winter on the Ming Wall at Jinshanling.

PAGES 112–13 | Ladies of the court. Tang figurines. Shaanxi Provincial Museum and Musée Guimet, Paris, donated by Jacques Polain. Photo by Roger Asselberghe.

Three figurines. The two in the foreground are of terra-cotta, the one in the background of painted wood.

PAGE 114 | Encampment on the Mongolian steppe.

PAGE 115 | **The Great Wall in spring at Huanghuacheng, north of Beijing.**

This location was once known as Huanghualu, "Path of the Yellow Flowers." It runs from Gubeikou in the east to Juyongguan in the west, near Mutianyu, and was built under the Ming dynasty. Most of it is built of stone, though there are a few brick sections.

PAGE 118 | **Polo player. Terra-cotta of the Tang dynasty. Private collection.**

The horse is at full gallop. The horseman, wearing a topknot, holds the reins with one hand and tries to hit the ball with the other. Polo was a very popular sport in China, introduced from Persia via the Silk Road, during or just before the Tang dynasty. It was played as far afield as Korea and Japan. Polo, whose Chinese name is *maqiu*, "horse ball," was played with curved sticks ending in crescent moon shapes, and the goals were made of netting.

PAGE 119 | **The Great Wall at Mutianyu.**

PAGES 122–23 | **Landscape in the Altai, Mongolia. Lake Achüt Nuur.**

PAGES 124–25 | **Kirghiz encampment, Afghan Pamir.**

The felt tents of the Kirghiz, *kirghas* or *ak-ui*, are traditional and perfectly adapted to their environment. They are similar to the tents used by almost all the nomads of central Asia, which the Mongols call *ger* and the Kazakhs *yurt*. A tent consists of a wooden framework covered with felt sheeting. The interior is huge, large enough to hold a whole family, guests, and young animals. Brightly colored woolen carpets, chests, and various utensils, folded bedding, and food (mainly milk, dried milk, and cream) are arranged in an immutable order. This form of dwelling has been used for centuries. Chinese princesses given in marriage to a barbarian ruler to cement an alliance were forced to adapt to this lifestyle and forget life at the imperial court.

PAGE 126 | **Turkoman women in their yurt, Afghan Turkestan.**

"To his strange tents I was carried With fleeces their walls are hung. Only mutton for food, and the milk of

mares!… Endless my exile, useless my tears" (see text on pages 116 and 117).

PAGE 127 | **Kazakh from the Altai, Mongolia.**

PAGE 129 | **Lady of the court. Terra-cotta of the Tang dynasty. Height: 13.5 in. (35 cm). Private collection.**

PAGE 130 | **The Great Wall at Huanghuacheng, seen from Zhuangdaokou, north of Beijing.**

This location, east of Juyongguan and west of Gubeikou, was also called Huangnilu and then Huanghuazhen. It is a mountain pass of strategic importance that controlled three routes from the north near Beijing, so it has a group of fortifications built under the Ming dynasty. Over a distance of around five miles there are forty-four signaling towers (*ditai*) and six bastions (*chengbao*). The reservoir now located to the east of the pass was built using many stones removed from the nearby wall.

PAGE 131 | **Terraces under cultivation at the foot of the Great Wall north of Beijing, at Wangquanyu.** *(See p. 94.)*

PAGE 132 | **Young Kazakh musician, Mongolia.**

She is playing the *dambura* (*dongbula* in the Chinese transcription used in Xinjiang), a type of long-necked lute or cithera, with frets and two strings. This type of instrument is to be found among most of the peoples of central Asia, especially in the sedentary populations.

PAGE 133 | **A shaft of light in the Mongolian steppe.**

PAGE 134 | **Detail of a fifteenth-century Turkish-Mongolian miniature, from the Album of the Conqueror. Topkapi Museum, Istanbul, Turkey.**

PAGE 135 | **The Great Wall at Simatai.** *(See p. 5.)*

PAGE 136 | **Bodhisattva, Yungang cave near Datong, Shanxi.**

This site is located on the southern aspect of Mount Wuchou and the Wuchou Pass, between the interior and exterior walls of the Han Wall. The *Hanshu* (History of the Han) explains that the Wuchou Pass was crossed several times by thousands of Xiongnu. It is a treasure trove of Buddhist art, the first Yungang caves having been sculpted under the Northern Wei dynasty (386–534), founded by the Tobas, a people who came from the north, and who were a branch of the Xian barbarians from the shores of the Argun, a tributary of the High Amur. The Northern Wei established their capital at Datong (Pingcheng), then later at Luoyang (now Henan), merging several Chinese and barbarian peoples in a decisive phase for the future formation of the Tang empire. Buddhism, which had been imported from central Asia, became the official religion. The head in the illustration is that of a bodhisattva (on the western side) who accompanies the central figure of the Buddha in cave no. 3, the largest in the series. The central Buddha is 45 feet (14 m) high, and the bodhisattvas on either side are 20 feet (6 m) high. The cave and the sculptures date in part from the "second period" of Yungang (465–494). They were left unfinished under the Northern Wei and are believed to have been completed under the Sui or more probably under the Tang. *Yungang shiku* (The Caves of Yungang) (Peking, 1977).

PAGE 137 | **Pagodas of the Silver Mountain (Yinshan Baota), north of Beijing.**

Built during the Liao, Qidan "barbarian" (907–1119), Jin, and Nuzhen "barbarian" (1115–1234) periods.

PAGES 138–39 | **The Great Wall at Heituo Shan, north of Beijing.**

PAGES 140–41 | **Bas-reliefs in the "Cloud Terrace" in the Juyongguan (Juyong Pass).**

The "Cloud Terrace" was built from 1343 through 1345 during the reign of the last Yuan emperor, Toghan Temur (1333–1367). It was originally "a pagoda overlooking the road" (*guojie ta*) inspired by the *chörten* gates that often marked the entrance to monastic complexes or cities in Tibet. Certain architectural features of this monument are evidence of the presence of the Tibetan style in China, favored during the reign of Qubilai (or Khubilai, 1260–1294), as a result of the close union, in the fields of politics and religion, between the new Mongolian rulers and Tibetan Buddhism.

All that remains of the structure is the rectangular base. The angular design of the gate is inspired by that of the city gates built before the Song period, so that the ceiling vault of the passage would have been trapezoidal in section. The building is massive in shape, topped with a white marble balustrade and decorated with numerous sculptures. According to reconstitutions suggested by experts such as the Japanese Murata and Fujieda, and the Chinese Su Bai, there were three *chörten* over the doorway. This arrangement of *chörten*, arranged on the same lowest level, suggests various interpretations, the number three referring to the Three Jewels or Three Buddhas.

The Ming, who were more traditional, returning to more Chinese concepts of architecture, replaced the *chörten* in 1448 with a wooden pavilion, of which the bases of the columns can still be seen. Even though the gate was remodeled, it remains typical of Yuan architecture and sculpture, inspired by Tibetan and Nepalese originals.

The arch of the door is framed by sculptures, faithful representations of the "Gates of Glory" of the Indian world, topped by a *garuda* (mythical sacred bird) fighting snakes. The walls inside the passage are carved with inscriptions in six languages—Sanskrit, Tibetan, Mongolian, Han Chinese, Uigur, and Tangut (Xixia)—evidence of the ecumenism of the Yuan. These inscriptions extol the virtues of those who erected a stupa and narrate the Buddhist legend of the golden elephant. The carvings around the door also include four large Chinese-style panels dedicated to the four kings who are the guardians of the regions of space. (Paola Mortari Vergara, "L'architecture de style tibétain en Chine. Epoque Yuan [1261–1367]," in *Demeures des hommes, sanctuaires des dieux* [Rome: Universita di Roma "La Sapienza," 1987].)

Under the Ming, changes were made to the monument, the pavilion, and the sculptures of the marble balustrade, and it was named Shitai Yunge, "Pavilion of the Clouds of the Stone Terrace," hence the name by which it is now known, "Cloud Terrace" (*yuntai*).

PAGE 142 | **The Great Wall at Heituo Shan, north of Beijing.**

The Mutianyu wall lies forty-five miles north of Beijing and seventeen miles from Huairou. It is south-southeast of the Heituo Shan.

This wall was built under the Ming and follows the peaks of the southern Yan Shan range. These constructions that run from north to south are spectacular, since they follow the line of steep slopes, making them as daring as they were superfluous in such a tortured landscape.

PAGE 143 | **Detail of a painting of the Yuan period,** *The Emperor Koubilai out Hunting.* © National Palace Museum, Taipei.

PAGE 145 | **Lassooing a horse. Mongolia, twentieth century.**

PAGES 146–47 | **The Great Wall at Jinshanling.**

PAGE 148 | **Detail of a painting of the Ming period.** © National Palace Museum, Taipei.

Qiu Ying is a painter who lived during the Ming dynasty. He came from Taicang (now Jiangsu) and died in 1552. He was famous for his faithful reproductions of the work of previous great artists such as Li Zhaodao (Tang dynasty) and Zhao Boju (Song dynasty), "not only transmitting their technique but also the beauty of their work." He labored with such concentration "that he heard neither drums nor trumpets, nor even the noise of the crowd, and did not even shed a glance over the walls at the women" (Oswald Siren, *The Chinese on the Art of Painting* [Peiping: Henri Vetch, 1937]).

PAGE 149 | **The Great Wall near the Huanghuacheng reservoir, north of Beijing.**

PAGE 150 | **Detail of a painting of the Yuan period.** © National Palace Museum, Taipei.

Zhao Mengfu (1254–1322) was a government minister, poet, and painter who was born in Zhejiang. Although he was related to the Song imperial family, he placed himself at the service of the Mongol emperor (Yuan dynasty). He proved to be deeply attached to the ancient tradition of painting, but he is better known as a calligrapher than as a painter. "The most important quality in painting is the spirit of the olden days. If it is not present, the work is not worth much, even if it is executed with skill. . . . My paintings seem to be simple and created swiftly, but true connoisseurs will realise that they are based on older models and for this reason they can be considered to be good." Zhao Mengfu's favorite classical subject matter was that of the Song dynasty and, even more so, the Tang dynasty. Han Gan was his favorite painter of horses (see p. 214), and horses were a favorite subject of his, which must have greatly pleased the Mongols.

The Mongols understood little of Chinese culture, and painting in particular, but they shared their love of horses. Horses had been a popular subject of paintings since the Tang dynasty. No doubt it was to interest or gain favor with their new masters that Chinese painters of the Yuan period particularly developed this aspect of their art.

Ren Renfa is another painter of horses of the Yuan period. Little is known about him, except that he came from the south. His most famous painting is *Horses at Pasture* (Victoria and Albert Museum, London), depicting a group of men and horses and demonstrating the mastery of a sophisticated technique.

PAGES 150–51 | **Ramparts at Pingyao, Shanxi Province.**

Pingyao lies south of Taiyuan. Although it is a long way from the northern frontier of Shanxi Province, it is a good example of a fortified city and is still well preserved. Built in 1370, in the reign of the emperor Hongwu, it was later expanded under the emperors Ming, Jiajing, and Wanli, then under the Qing. Its bankers had the reputation of being prosperous. The brick perimeter wall is four miles long and in places it is about forty feet high and eighteen feet thick. There are seventy-two watchtowers (*ditu*) on the exterior, placed every eighteen feet, and there is a tower at each of the four corners.

PAGE 152 | **Civil servant of the Qing dynasty. Late-nineteenth-century photographic montage. Collection of Michel Culas, Paris.**

The face of the civil servant has been inserted on a painted background showing him seated on a thronelike chair and dressed in the official uniform (*bufu*) adorned with gold and silk embroidery. His rank is shown in the "mandarin square" (*buzi* or *beixiong*) that he wears on his chest and back. The practice of identifying the rank of such an official dates from the start of the Ming dynasty, when the grade of civil servants was shown on their clothing in the form of a bird. An official of the first rank wore a white crane, then came a golden pheasant, peacock, wild goose, silver pheasant, egret, mandarin duck, golden oriole, and bird of paradise. The rank of high-ranking army officers was shown in the form of a wild animal—in descending order, a lion (later a unicorn), leopard, tiger, black bear, panther, spotted bear, rhinoceros, and sea horse.

The scholar–civil servant class began to be formed as early as the Han dynasty. It made itself indispensable to the autocratic power and ran the empire as a centralized and cumbersome bureaucracy. Under several dynasties there was bitter rivalry between the scholars and the court eunuchs.

This class was of necessity but also by its nature subject to the will of the emperor, even though mention should be made of certain brave individuals who dared to remonstrate with the monarch. A smart statesman would suggest that the emperor take a particular course of action in such as way as to permit the emperor to believe he had thought of it himself, for only the emperor could be right, whether it concerned the building of a palace, a long canal, or a wall. Expressing reservations about what the emperor wanted was to endanger one's life, especially if one was in direct opposition. Such behavior would be interpreted as an attempt to usurp the throne, the most serious crime possible. The annals of the beginning of the Ming dynasty reveal stories of the tortures endured by those who menaced the throne, and they sound like a journey through hell itself. The "eighteen hells" depicted in Buddhist temples are a reminder of what was done during the Ming dynasty. Under the reign of these emperors—and Confucius had already said that "a brutal monarch is worse than a tiger"—the protection of a scholar represented a guarantee of survival.

PAGES 154–55 | A winter's day at the Imperial Palace, Beijing.

A view of the Taihe Dian (Room of Supreme Harmony) terrace looking south toward the Taihe Men (Gate of Supreme Harmony), with the Wu Men (Noon Gate) in the background. The Ming emperor Yongle rebuilt Beijing ("Capital of the North") near the site of the former capital city of the Yuan emperors. However, he created a new layout consisting of an inner city and an outer city. The inner city covered one block at the northern end, and the outer city covered a rectangle at the south end. Yongle also remodeled the interior palace, making it look as it does today.

PAGE 156 | Hanging Palace of the Green Cliff (Cangyan Shanqiao Loudian).

About twenty miles south of Jingxing (xing: a ravine or gorge) in the province of Hebei, famous for the battle between the Zhao and Han states in 205 B.C.E., is a crossing point and a route taken by invaders because it links the Taihang Shan range with the great northern plain.

The palace is built on a single arch straddling a ravine several dozen feet deep; it was built under the Sui and rebuilt under the Qing. It is topped by a double roof. It was once a place of worship and pilgrimage. (See also p. 178.)

PAGE 157 | Young Han girl, Autonomous Region of Ningxia.

PAGES 160–61 | The Great Wall at Mutianyu.

View showing examples of Ming military architecture. The structures attached to the wall (hollow towers and small dwellings), used to house soldiers, only appeared in the mid-sixteenth century, when the building work was performed under the supervision of Qi Jiguang, a general under the Ming and commander of the Jizhou garrison from 1567, who was commanded to build the wall from north of Beijing right to the sea.

PAGE 162 | The Yellow River in Shanxi. Ji Xian region, near Hu Kou.

PAGE 163 | The Yellow River and the Great Canal, detail of Ming map. Museum of the History of the Revolution, Beijing.

PAGES 164–65 | Rapids on the Yellow River at Hu Kou, Shanxi.

PAGE 168 | Han peasant in Shanxi.

(under Hongzhi). Other pavilions and external fortifications were built in 1506, during the reign of Zhengde, and in 1536, under Jiajing. Only the corner towers and gatehouses are made of brick.

Jiayuguan, its fortress, and the curtain walls that guard the approaches to it together comprise a good example of the Ming defense system, whose main features consisted of:

- *Guancheng:* A citadel associated with the defense of a pass. It could consist of an immense fortification, built to take advantage of the topography and with between two and four gates. The most typical citadels still in a good state of preservation (restored) are at Shanhaiguan and Jiayuguan.

- *Wengcheng,* or *yuecheng:* A curtain wall designed to protect the approaches to a gate and placed in front of it. The shape varies, depending on the terrain, and may be round, square, or rectangular.

- *Luocheng:* Another type of curtain wall, designed to protect the approaches to a citadel. It generally follows the line of the walls. It may be protected by a moat or ditch. Sometimes this term is used to denote a small fortification that is quite separate from the main fortress, in which case it may also be known as *waicheng.*

- *Fenghuotai:* A tall signaling tower used on the frontier from an early stage. The names changed depending on the era. Under the Han, they were known as *houtai* (usually used for a watchtower) or *tingsui;* under the Tang, *suitai;* under the Ming, *yantun* or *tuntai.* On high ground where the topography permitted they were erected at regular intervals, usually of ten *lis,* but sometimes less, if this was justified by the landscape.

After the Qin dynasty these towers became one of the main elements of the defense system of the wall and were used to indicate the imminent arrival of hostile forces. Signaling towers were built in front of, on top of, or behind the wall, thus creating a network of communications with the garrisons. The speed of transmission of information depended on the degree of efficiency of the system. The towers might be round or square and were built, like the wall, of compacted earth, brick, or stone, depending on their locations and the periods in question.

Cannons came into use during the Ming dynasty. A text dated 1466 specifies that "when one through one hundred men are espied, shoot one plume of smoke and one cannon blast; for five hundred men, two plumes of smoke and two cannon blasts; for more than a thousand, three plumes of smoke and three cannon blasts; more than five thousand, four plumes of smoke and four cannon blasts; ten thousand or more, five plumes of smoke and five cannon blasts."

PAGE 187 | **Young Mongol camel drover.**

PAGES 188–89 | **The Great Wall between Jinshanling and Simatai.**

PAGES 190–91 | **Two horsemen, painting from the Tang dynasty.** © National Palace Museum, Taipei.
  Painted by Wei Yan (early eighth century).

PAGES 192–93 | **Mongolia of the steppes.**

PAGES 194–95 | **Horses in the Mongolian steppe. Bayan Ölgi.**

PAGES 196–97 | **Kazakh with his trained eagle, Altai Mountains, Mongolia.**
  Hunting, in this case with a trained eagle, was once a training exercise for combat but is also a source of income and a sport. Hunting with a trained eagle makes it possible to captured furred game such as foxes, hares, and marmots.

  The style of animal sculpture found in the Altai Mountains, produced by the nomads of central Asia, and especially the Kazakhs, often features the eagle, sometimes in conjunction with a griffon.

PAGES 200–201 | **The Great Wall at Jinshanling, near Linchang.**

PAGE 202 | **The Great Wall at Jinshanling.**

PAGE 203 | Terra-cotta figurine of the Tang period. Private collection.

PAGE 204 | Prunus blossom.

PAGE 205 | **Young Han girl in Shanxi.**

PAGES 208–9 | **Bridge over the Wuding River, Shaanxi.**

The Wuding River is a tributary of the middle Yellow River. The cities connected with barbarian invasions or the Great Wall lie upstream of this river and the other tributaries that pass through the loess terrain southeast of the Ordos. These include the cities of Yulin ("Elm Forest"), on the Yulin He to the north, which was an important garrison under the Tang, Song, and Ming dynasties, and held markets for trading horses, furs, leather, and camelhair for tea, salt, and other items useful to the Mongols; and Hengshan, southwest of Yulin. At Tongwan (later known as Xiazhou), thirty miles to the northwest, on the upper reaches of the Wuding and near the frontier with Inner Mongolia, in a region that is now desert, lie the ruins of the former capital of the Xia, one of the barbarian states that ruled this region from 407 through 431. Tongwan remained an important fortification under the Northern Wei. The first emperor ordered the construction of part of the wall on the right bank of the Wuding River between Shangjing (now Yuhebu) and Suide.

There is another fortress near Yulin, three miles to the north, called Zhenbeitai. It takes the form of a four-story tower 100 feet high, built in 1607 in the reign of the Ming emperor Wanli. It was built to house the garrison that supervised the horse fair (*mashi*) at Hongshan ("Red Mountain") that was attached to Yulin. Horses were traded between officials of the empire and the nomads who lived outside the wall (*guanwai*). The fortress backs onto the wall at Hongshan.

Under the Tang, the emperor Xuanzong permitted such trading with the Turks (Tujue) at Ximanjiang (now Inner Mongolia) in exchange for gold.

Under the Song, horses were bartered for tea. For example, from 1045 through 1160, 116,000 horses were traded for silk, tea, and silver. Under the Ming emperor

Yongle, trading took place mainly in Gansu, and then in the northeast with the Nuzhen people. During the reign of the Ming emperor Wanli, at Xuanfu (now Xuanhua) about 18,000 horses were traded for 120,000 liang of silver annually. At Datong, 10,000 horses were traded for 70,000 liang of silver annually, and at Shanxi 6,000 horses were traded against 40,000 liang. This official trade in horses, through the imperial administration, was eventually discontinued. Thanks to its location at the northern end of the loess plateau, close to the steppe of the Ordos, Yulin has always been a point of contact between the traditional world of the Han Chinese and the nomads.

The first wall in the region was built on the western frontier by the Kingdom of Wei, to protect itself against Qin, in 361 B.C.E. King Zhaowang of Qin built a wall that ran close to Yulin to protect his land against the nomads. Qin Shi Huangdi restored the wall built by his ancestor. Under the Han dynasty, the Xiongnu were pushed back northward; consequently, this section of the wall fell into disrepair and was forgotten. Under the Ming, Yulin, then called Yansui, became one of the major frontier garrisons (*jiu bianzhen*). Walls that are visible to this day were built around the city. Yu Zujun, a scholar from Zhejiang, moved to Yulin and lived there from 1471. He applied a policy toward the Mongols that mixed conciliatory and defensive measures, especially by obtaining permission from the court to build the first walls in the Ordos.

PAGES 210–11 | **The Mongolian steppe at the foot of the Altai Mountains.**

PAGE 212 | **The Great Wall at Jinshanling.**

PAGE 213 | **Guan Yu, guardian of the frontiers, in the Pule Si (late eighth century) at Chengde, Hebei.**

At Chengde, in Hebei, Pule Si, "Temple of Universal Joy," is dominated by the bronze statue of Guan Yu (or Guan Di, Guan Gong, or Wu Di), god of war, guardian of the passes and the frontiers. He was originally a general, hero of the historical novel, *The Three Kingdoms*, the sworn brother of Zhang Fei and Liu Bei, a native of Jiexian (now Linyi) in southwest Shanxi Province. He was captured by the enemy and executed in 219. Considered to be the most

260

famous and bravest of the Chinese military heroes, he was deified under the Ming and called by the emperor "Pillar of the Sky and Protector of the Kingdom," becoming one of the most popular gods in China; many temples were dedicated to him. He was the patron saint of soldiers, but also of sellers of soybeans (this had been his occupation in his youth) and other lucrative occupations. He eventually was also made the god of wealth and even of literature, because he was said to be able to recite the whole of the *Zuozhuan* by heart (Jacques Dars, notes, "Au bord de l'eau [Beside the Water]," Bibliothèque de la Pléiade [Paris: Gallimard, 1978]).

PAGE 214 | *Groom and Horses,* **painting of the Tang period.** © **National Palace Museum, Taipei.**

This painting, attributed to Han Gan (ca. 720–780), represents two prancing horses, one black, the other white, the latter being ridden by a sturdy horseman who has foreign features. The horse in the foreground wears a richly decorated, attention-catching saddle. The general effect is one of power, with a subtle, muted color scheme. The horses are lively, the horseman looks ferocious. The impression is of subjugated vitality, cunningly conveyed by the painter. All the nobility of these racehorses is captured in the drawing—the line of the neck, the clip-clopping of the hooves, the pricking up of the ears into the wind.

Han Gan was a painter who lived under the Tang dynasty. He came from Yantian, in what is now Shaanxi, and studied under Cao Pa (ca. 720), who belonged to the entourage around the emperor Xuanzong (713–756). He became the protégé of the poet Wang Wei (699–759) and obtained favors from the emperor. Although his talent led him to take an interest in a variety of subject matter, including human figures, flowers, and frescoes for Buddhist temples, he is considered one of the greatest equestrian painters of China. "When Han Gan paints a horse, he himself becomes a horse," wrote Su Shi (1036–1101), one of the members of the class of "gentleman painters" under the Northern Song dynasty. He painted the emperor's favorite white horse, Zhaoyebai, "a streak of light in the dark," and the emperor examining his horses, stag-hunting, or leaving for a night excursion. Han Gan's work also includes a portrait of Yang Guifei (718–756), the favorite of the emperor

Xuanzong, climbing into the saddle to re-create the famous theme of the history of the Han princess Zhaojun, who was given in marriage to Huhanye, king of the Xiongnu, in 33 B.C.E. The moment during the story when, surrounded by her escort, who are part Xiongnu, part Chinese, Zhaojun is about to climb into the saddle and leave the land of civilization for the land of the barbarians has inspired numerous poems and plays, especially under the Yuan and Ming dynasties. Among the most famous are "Fall in the Palace of the Han" (*Hangong qiu*) by Ma Cheyuan and "The Departure of Zhaojun for the Frontier" (*Zhaojun chusai*) by Chen Yujiao. In Han Gan's interpretation, Zhaojun is replaced by Yang Guifei.

The poems inspired by the destiny of the concubine exiled under the Han include one by Li Panlung (who lived during the Ming period in the sixteenth century) entitled "Zhaojun" (*La Poésie chinoise,* trans. Patricia Guillermaz [Paris: Seglers, 1957]).

The wind is cold on the snow of the Celestial Mountains.
I take my cithara that I play on horseback.
When my song is ended, I forget that the moon shines on
*   the Blue Lake [Koukou Nor]*
I contemplate it as if I still wandered through the
*   Han palace.*

PAGE 215 | **The Great Wall at Badaling (restored).**

The construction is typical of the Ming period, seen on the inside. It is built of stone with crenellations on the exterior and gargoyles on the interior. This part of the wall is north of Juyongguan and is ten miles (16 km) long. It is the closest to the capital, at only about thirty miles (48 km) northwest of Beijing, which gives it strategic importance in the foreground, at the entrance to the natural passages over the Mongolian plateau across the Yan Shan range, to the east and the Taihang Shan to the north, with the northern plain in the west.

This natural passage is formed by a fast-flowing mountain stream (*guangou,* the Torrent of the Pass) between steep, rocky peaks that become higher as they approach the fortified site of Badaling. Strategists have always considered it to be a "formidable barrier, yesterday and today, to control South and North" (*kong'e nanbei zhi gujin jufang*). Gao She, poet of the frontiers under the Tang dynasty, describes, with the emphasis of a scholar traveling into wild country, how as he penetrates deeper into the Juyong Pass, "inaccessible slopes down which water flows, among the peaks the clouds are high in the sky."

The name of the pass was used as long ago as the period of the Fighting Kingdoms. The name Juyongguan is said to mean "Pass in Which the Common Folk Live," a reference to the peasants brought in to clear the terrain under the first emperor, Qin Shi Huangdi. It has been given a variety of names down the centuries, including Xiguan (Pass of the West), under the Three Kingdoms; Nakuanguan (Pass of Tribute-offering), under the Northern Qi; and Jimenguan, then Jundouguan, under the Tang. But after the Liao dynasty, it once again became Juyongguan, and has remained so.

Before the Ming dynasty, fortifications were erected in the pass to ensure that it was better controlled but without an elaborate system of defenses. When Genghis Khan managed to push through the "Neck of the Gulley" (Cabciyal, the Mongol name for Jiayuguan) in 1211, the wall no longer existed, even if, according to Chinese tradition, entry was gained by means of a trick. Under the Yuan dynasty, two monumental gates marked the two ends of the pass. A building (*guojie ta*, a pagoda straddling the road) that had no military purpose was built in the pass. It was remodeled under the Ming, and was known as the *yuntai* (Cloud Terrace, see ill. pp. 140 and 141).

The first Ming fortifications, the beginning of the complex of walls and bastions of which numerous features still remain, extended from south of the pass (Nankou) northward to Badaling, and were built between 1370 and the sixteenth century, especially after the defeat of Tumu in 1450.

PAGE 218 | **The Great Wall at Simatai.**

PAGE 219 | **Sculpture of the Northern Wei period. Private collection.**

PAGE 220 | **The Great Wall in winter at Simatai.**

PAGE 221 | **A Kazakh from the Altai Mountains of Mongolia.**

PAGE 223 | **Kirghiz caravan in the Afghan Pamir.**

PAGE 224 | **Fresco of the Tang period in Shaanxi Province.**
Hunting on horseback. Tomb of Prince Zhang Huai, Qian Xian district.

PAGES 224–25 | **The fortress of Zhenbeipu at Ningxia.**
The land on the left bank of the Yellow River, close to the modern city of Yinchuan, between the water and the Helan Shan range, is irrigated. The region is naturally prosperous but has a scattering of steppes or desert regions. The area has always been bitterly disputed by the nomadic barbarians and the sedentary Han. South of the Helan Shan range, which runs almost north-south and constitutes a natural barrier, the Great Wall was built under the first emperor right up to the Yellow River to the south. Several fortresses such as Zhenbeipu were built on the eastern slopes of the Helan Shan, under the Ming. The wall has been used as a film location, which explains the presence of the standards ripped to shreds by the wind.

page 226–27. **The Great Wall at Jinshanling.**

Selective Bibliography

ANDERSON, Aenas. *Relation de voyage de Lord Macartney à la Chine dans les années 1792, 1793, 1794.* Paris: Aubier-Montaigne, 1978.

BADDELEY, John F. *Russia, Mongolia, China.* London: Macmillan, 1919.

BAILLY, Jean-Sylvain. *Lettres sur l'Atlantide de Platon et sur l'histoire ancienne de l'Asie.* Paris: Debure Frères, 1779.

BELL, John. *A Journey from St Petersburg to Peking, 1719–22.* New York: Barnes and Noble, 1966.

BERTHELOT, André. *L'Asie ancienne centrale et sud-orientale d'après Ptolémée.* Paris: Payot, 1930.

BOORSTIN, Daniel. *Les Découvreurs.* Paris: Robert Laffont, 1986.

BRAND, Adam. *Relation du voyage de Mr Ever Isbrand envoyé de sa majesté czarienne à l'empereur de la Chine en 1692, 93 et 94.* Amsterdam, 1699.

CAGNAT, René, and Michel JAN. *Le Milieu des Empires.* 2d ed. Paris: Robert Laffont, 1990.

Changcheng baike qinshu (Encyclopedia of the Great Wall). *Zhongguo changcheng xuehui, Jilin renmin chubanshe,* 1994.

CLAUDEL, Paul. *Connaissance de l'Est.* Paris: Gallimard, 1974.

DEMIÉVILLE, Paul, ed. *Anthologie de la poésie chinoise classique.* Paris: Gallimard, 1962.

DOOLITTLE, Justus. *Social Life of the Chinese.* New York: Harper Brothers, 1867.

DUHALDE, Jean-Baptiste. *Description géographique, historique, chronologique, physique et politique de la Chine et de la Tartarie.* La Haye: H. Scheurleer, 1735.

ÉTIEMBLE, René. *Connaissons-nous la Chine?* Paris: Gallimard, 1964.

GAO Wang. *Bolan changcheng fengcai.* Beijing, 1991.

_____. *Neimenggu changcheng shihua.* Huhehuote, 1991.

_____. *Changcheng fanggu wanlixing.* Beijing, 1991.

GERNET, J. *La Vie quotidienne en Chine à la veille de l'invasion mongole, 1250–1276.* Paris: Hachette, 1959.

GIBERT, Lucien. *Dictionnaire historique et géographique de la Mandchourie.* Hong Kong, 1934.

GILBERT DE VOISINS, Auguste. *Écrit en Chine.* Paris: You-Feng, 1987.

GRANET, Marcel. *La civilisation chinoise.* Paris: Albin Michel, 1968.

_____. *La Pensée chinoise,* Paris: Albin Michel, 1968.

GROUSSET, René. *L'empire des steppes*. Paris: Payot, 1965.

GUILLERMAZ, Patricia. *La Poésie chinoise*. Paris: Seghers, 1957.

GUO Moruo, ed. *Zhongguo shigao dituji*. 2 vols. Shanghai, 1996.

Hebei sheng pudong dituji. Beijing, 1994.

HIRTH, F. *China and the Roman Orient*. Shanghai/Hong Kong, 1885.

Histoire secrète des Mongols. Translated and edited by Marie-Dominique EVEN and Rodica POP. Paris: Gallimard, 1994.

HUC, Régis-Évariste. *Souvenirs d'un voyage dans la Tartarie et le Thibet*. L'Astrolabe—Peuples du Monde, 1987.

JETTMAR, Karl. *L'Art des steppes*. Paris: Albin Michel, 1964.

KADARE, Ismail. *La Grande Muraille*. Paris: Fayard, 1993.

KAFKA, Franz. *The Great Wall of China and Other Short Stories*. Penguin, 1993.

KAIKO, Takeshi. *La Muraille de Chine*. Paris: Philippe Picquier, 1992.

LARRIEU, Abbé. *La Grande Muraille de Chine*. Paris: Ernest Leroux, 1887.

LATTIMORE, Owen. *Inner Asian Frontiers of China*. Hong Kong: Oxford University Press, 1988.

Lettres édifiantes et curieuses de Chine par les missionnaires jésuites, 1702–1776. Garnier-Flammarion, 1979.

LEYS, Simon. *Essais sur la Chine*. Paris: Robert Laffont, 1998.

LIN Yutang. *La Chine et les Chinois*. 1936. Reprint, Paris: Payot, 1997.

LUO Zhewen and ZHAO Luo. *The Great Wall of China in History and Legend*. Beijing: Foreign Languages Press, 1986.

MANKALL, Mark. *Russia and China*. Cambridge, Mass.: Harvard University Press, 1971.

MARGOULIES, G. *Anthologie raisonnée de la littérature chinoise*. Paris: Payot, 1948.

MARTINI, Martino. *Atlas Sinensis*. Amsterdam, 166–.

MASPERO, Henri. *La Chine antique*. Paris: Presses universitaires de France, 1965.

NAGEL (Guide). *Chine*. Geneva, 1967.

NEEDHAM, Joseph. *La Science chinoise et l'Occident*. Paris: Seuil, 1973.

POLO, Marco. *Description of the World*. Translated and with introduction by A. C. Moule and Paul Pelliot. London: Routledge, 1938.

ROSSABI, Morris. *China and Inner Asia, from 1368 to the Present Day*. London: Thames and Hudson, 1975.

SEGALEN, Victor. *Œuvres complètes*. Paris: Robert Laffont, 1995.

SIMA Qian. *Historical Records*. Translated by Raymond Dawson. Oxford University Press, 1994.

STEIN, Sir Aurel. *Ruins of Desert Cathay*. 2 vols. Macmillan, 1912.

SYKES, General Sir Percy. *The Quest for Cathay*. London: A & C. Black, 1938.

TAN Qixiang, ed. *Zhongguo lishi dituji*. 8 vols., Shanghai, 1982.

TEILHARD DE CHARDIN, Pierre. *Lettres de voyage*. Paris: Grasset, 1956.

TOYNBEE, Arnold. *A Study of History*. Oxford: Oxford University Press, 1987.

TU Fu. *Selected Poems*. Peking: Foreign Languages Press, 1964.

VERBIEST, Ferdinand. *Voyages de l'empereur de la Chine dans la Tartarie*. Paris: Estienne Michallet, 1685.

VOLTAIRE. *Dictionnaire de la pensée de Voltaire*. Edited by André Versaille. Éditions Complexe, 1994.

WALDRON, Arthur. *The Great Wall of China: From History to Myth*. Cambridge: Cambridge University Press, 1990. Contains an extensive bibliography.

XU Yuanzhong. *Song of the Immortals: An Anthology of Classical Chinese Poetry*. Beijing: New World Press, 1994.

XU Yuanzhong, LOH Beiyei, and WU Juntao. *Three Hundred Tang Poems*. Hong Kong: Commercial Press, 1996.

YOUNGHUSBAND. *Heart of a Continent*. London: John Murray, 1896. Reprint, Hong Kong: Oxford University Press, 1984.

YULE, Henry, and Henri CORDIER. *Cathay and the Way Thither*. 4 vols. London: Hakluyt Society, 1913–16.

Index

*Page numbers of photographs are represented in **bold**.*

Acknowledgments

MICHEL JAN
dedicates the text of this book to the
memory of Jacques Gillermaz,
with whom he extensively discussed
the content of this project before his untimely
death in 1998.
He is particularly grateful to Professor Paul Bady,
of the University of Paris VI–Denis-Diderot,
for his suggestions and corrections.

ROLAND AND SABRINA MICHAUD
would like to thank the following
for their valuable assistance:
Ji Dahai and Huang Xinghua, Anne and Pierre Barroux,
Hervé and Alice de Malliard, Jean-Yves Merlet,
and Pascale Vacher.
They are particularly grateful to
Francis Deron and Odile Pierquin
for having initiated them into
the Chinese world and culture.
They would also like to thank Daniel Chocu
for his patience and excellent color photogravure,
and Romain Michaud, who took the photograph
on page 85. Roland and Sabrina Michaud
are members of the Leica Foundation.

This book
was typeset in 11.5 point Albertina MT
and produced on 170 g JOB MATT paper
The photogravure was produced
by the Imprimerie Nationale, Paris

Printed in France